Any fool may write a most valuable book by chance, if he will only tell us what he heard and saw with veracity.
Thomas Gray (1716-71)

Remember that, as a teenager, you are at the last stage in your life when you will be happy to hear that the phone is for you.
Fran Lebowitz, *Social Studies* (1981)

ECHOES OF '69

Stephen Howard Jones

First Published 2003

This book is copyright under the Berne Convention. All rights are reserved. Apart from any fair dealing for the purpose of private study, research, criticism or review, as permitted under the Copyright Act 1956, no part of this publication may be reproduced, stored in a retrieval system, or transmitted in any form or by any means electronic, electrical, chemical, mechanical, optical, photocopying, recording or otherwise without the prior permission of the copyright owner. Enquiries should be sent to the publisher at the undermentioned address.

S.H.Jones
11 Fairview Close
Chadderton
Oldham
OL9 9UZ

© Stephen Howard Jones 2003

The right of Stephen Howard Jones to be recognised as the author of this work has been asserted

ISBN: 0 9545559 0 2

Printed by Newton Printing Ltd of London
www.newtonprinting.com

For Gregory: who spends every day bursting towards tomorrow and filling my life with smiles.

For Lynn: for her love, unswerving support, cheer-leading and proof-reading.

For Mum and Dad: without whom...!!!

ACKNOWLEDGEMENTS

The author would like to acknowledge the invaluable assistance provided by the following people without whom the project and process would have been a complete and utter shambles:

My wife, Lynn and son, Greg, for putting up with me generally.

Andy Searle at The Parrs Wood Press, Manchester for his advice, encouragement and publishing acumen.

The late Tom Nichol at Rochdale A.F.C. for his enthusiastic input to my research.

Richard Catlow and Dave Appleton, at the Rochdale Observer, for their interest and support.

Reg Jenkins for providing both the foreword and the opportunity to talk to one of my boyhood heroes.

Josie Ashworth (widow of Joe), Judith Hilton (daughter of Fred Ratcliffe), Rob Sunderland and Dave Butterworth for the generous loan of valuable archive material and photographs.

My grateful thanks to all of you.

CONTENTS

ABOUT THE AUTHOR 8
FOREWORD by Reg Jenkins 9

1. Introduction 11
2. July 1968 15
3. August 1968 23
4. September 1968 38
5. October 1968 52
6. November 1968 62
7. December 1968 76
8. January 1969 87
9. February 1969 97
10. March 1969 107
11. April 1969 120
12. May 1969 134
13. Aftermath 144

APPENDIX 1 Where are they now? 151
APPENDIX 2 The Statistics 157

ABOUT THE AUTHOR

Steve Jones is a 47 year old accountant now living in Chadderton, Lancashire. He spent his first twenty-one years as a resident of Rochdale surviving various character-moulding experiences such as; being the son of a well-known local policeman; pushing a heavily-laden market trolley up Toad Lane numerous times per day as part of his "Saturday Job"; a particularly arduous Sunday paper-round which took in the local Remand Centre, Buckley Hall; and several near-death experiences with Chester's Mild and Boddington's Bitter. After successfully avoiding expulsion from each of his schools (Halifax Road Primary, Howarth Cross High and Greenhill Upper), he set off, four A-levels tucked under his arm, to Manchester Polytechnic to read Accountancy, Playboy and Beer Mats. Graduating, exhausted, four years later, he took up a "proper job" with the North Western Electricity Board before realising, eight months later, that playing office cricket with a rolled-up newspaper was not actually advancing his career. A variety of senior European finance roles followed, embracing the manufacture of products as varied as Bryan Robson's football boots, PVC safety gloves, T-cut and Toilet seats and somewhere along the way he managed to marry the love of his life, Lynn, the union of which contrived to produce a "mini-Steve" named Greg(ory), now twelve years old.

Unexpected redundancy in the immediate aftermath of the 9/11 tragedy saw Steve with time on his hands and "Echoes of '69" was his excuse to get out of the ironing duties at home.

A staunch supporter of his home-town football team until leaving Rochdale in 1977, Steve (and Greg) now split their allegiance between Manchester United and "the Dale", with Steve regularly contributing articles to the match programme "The Voice of Spotland". This is his first entry into the literary world and allows his new work colleagues at Michelin Services Limited to take the piss mercilessly.

FOREWORD

When Steve approached me to write a few words about this book, I was delighted to accept. Season 1968/69, on which the book is based, was a momentous one for the Club and indeed for me personally. Reading Steve's account of the ups and downs of the season brought back many happy memories and his tales of growing up in the Rochdale of that era had me laughing out loud at many of the passages.

I still have many fond memories of my time at Rochdale F.C., both for the Club and for the people of the town, and I can thoroughly recommend the book as a humorous reminder of the Dale's "glory season".

All the best and "Up the Dale" !

Reg Jenkins.

1.

INTRODUCTION

There should be an invention that bottles up a memory like perfume, and it never faded, never got stale, and whenever I wanted to I could uncork the bottle, and live the memory all over again.
Daphne Du Maurier, *Rebecca* (1938)

From the outset, the aim of these ramblings was to provide a cathartic outpouring for a self-confessed football "nutter" who would characterise his role in life by reference to the following list of priorities (in descending order of importance):

1. Husband to Lynn and Dad to Gregory (aged 10).
2. Manchester United fanatic and Season-Ticket Holder.
3. Still-fond follower of Rochdale F.C. (when 2 - above - are away).
4. Avid collector of Football Programmes and memorabilia/ ephemera.
5. Enthusiastic spectator and self-styled connoisseur of Football Grounds.
6. Statistics compulsive (note the list only 40 words into the narrative!).
7. Accountant (!).

I suppose that, looking back, I had been pretty keen on football for some time but Season 1968/1969 represented a serious change in my spectating habits. I graduated from being an armchair follower of Manchester United, taken to occasional games by my Dad, to a

ECHOES OF '69

committed and dedicated Supporter of Rochdale A.F.C. ("The Dale"). As a typical twelve year-old undertaking that uneasy and challenging transition to "Becoming a Teenager", this football season represented a rite of passage; a truly formative year on a personal level, set against the backdrop of era-defining World events and massive developments in popular culture and music. Transcending all of this, however, was one cataclysmic occurrence;

THE DALE WERE PROMOTED

(For, at the time of writing, the one and only occasion in their frankly none-too-illustrious history!!!).

Sat here in front of my trusty PC some thirty-three years on, redundant and looking for a job for the first time in my adult life, my thoughts naturally turned introspective. Among other things, my memories kept flicking back to that time of innocence and, amazingly, I found myself almost absent-mindedly writing down the following list of names:

Chris HARKER
Graham SMITH   Colin PARRY   Joe ASHWORTH   Derek RYDER
Vinnie LEECH   Billy RUDD
Norman WHITEHEAD   Tony BUCK   Reg JENKINS   Dennis BUTLER

Old school friends? A firm of solicitors on The Esplanade in Rochdale?

No!!! These are the names of my erstwhile HEROES!!! Warriors in blue in my rose-tinted reminiscence. Men of the common people (unlike today's pampered Premiership stars who probably never meet a regular fan), these chaps helped to shape my young life.

Jenkins ("Big Reg"); the Club's record goal scorer, who always disported himself like a favourite uncle but was deadly in front of goal.

Ryder; the first time I had seen a man in tears as he was carried off on a stretcher after a painful injury in a match at Spotland.

INTRODUCTION

Parry; with whom my mate John Buckley and I sat, in absolute awe, on the bus (!!!) on the way to the final promotion-clinching match of the season against Southend United.

And **Melling**, who played a bit part during this season of seasons, but who was the first man I heard using seriously bad language (as the son of a policeman, I'd had a sheltered upbringing!). During the 4-1 win at Bradford Park Avenue, the ball came into the crowd where I was standing and Melling, anxious to add to the two goals he'd already scored, shouted "Chuck us that f***ing ball quick you tw*t!!! Naturally I (the tw*t in question) was honoured to accede to his command!

So why is it that these names spring readily from my memory when I can't even remember my own mobile phone number? What quirk of the human brain contrives to make me associate "copping a snog" with Beverley McKay with the postponement of Notts County (away)? As I pondered on this and other unanswerable questions (such as, why is there only **one** Monopolies Commission?; how do they get the non-stick coating to stick to the pan?; and what exactly did the first man to milk a cow **actually** think he was doing?) it occurred to me that it would be a cathartic and self-cleansing exercise to commit my thoughts to paper, or hard disk to be more precise. It would also keep me occupied whilst I was waiting for someone to re-employ a forty-six year old accountant and, at worst, it would be a legacy which I could hand to my ten year-old, Greg, and say, "That, my son, is what it was like to be thirteen in my day!!!". I can predict his first two questions now; "Dad, what's a bus and who are Bradford Park Avenue?". Callow youth!!

Consequently, what I'm going to do over the next few chapters is to take the reader through a chronological sequence of events from July 1968 to June 1969 by specific reference to Rochdale football club's historic season, and intersperse this with some personal anecdotes and references to contemporary social and cultural topics.

ECHOES OF '69

Rochdale - the town that, apparently, nobody knows. The town about which, in 1972, the then manager of Coventry City, one Noel Cantwell, said "Where's Rochdale?". This is fact! The same town which Prince Charles visited and decided to wear a "Davy Crockett" hat for the day. Evidently, on his return to Buckingham Palace, the Queen asked him why he had chosen this particular headgear and he said "Because you told me to do so, Mummy!". The Queen retorted that she had never so instructed him but Charles was adamant; "Don't you remember? I told you that I was going to Rochdale and I think you said "Wear the Fox Hat!" (This is made up!!!).

What it will NOT contain, unlike apparently every other publication pertaining to Rochdale which has ever been written, is ANY reference to the following:

1. Gracie Fields.
2. Cyril Smith.
3. The Co-operative Movement.
4. Clogs.
5. Shawls.
6. Cloth Caps.
7. Whippets.
8. Dark Satanic Mills.
9. Lisa Stansfield.

I sincerely hope that you'll enjoy reading it just half as much as I've enjoyed scribbling it!

2.

JULY 1968

Oh, he's football crazy, he's football mad
And the football it has robbed him o' the wee bit sense he had,
And it would take a dozen skivvies, his clothes to wash and scrub
Since our Jock became a member of that terrible football club.
Jimmie McGregor, *Football Crazy*, song from 1960

It had already been quite a momentous year. January had seen the launch of the mildly jingoistic "I'm Backing Britain" campaign (hands up anyone who remembers Hughie Green and Monica Rose?) which set the tone for the Nation. In the United States, people were becoming increasingly opposed to the Vietnam War as images of a prisoner being summarily executed by a bullet to the head filled our black and white television screens. There was civil unrest in many States as racial tensions boiled over following the assassination of Dr. Martin Luther King. In Paris, rioting students from the Sorbonne provided the catalyst for a General Strike which crippled France and almost brought about the downfall of De Gaulle and his government. This was the beginning of the end of the "Peace and Love" era of "The Swinging Sixties" as Bobby Kennedy was assassinated in Los Angeles and, worldwide, protests became increasingly militant - even the Beatles joined in as "Revolution" was issued as the B-side to "Hey Jude", the definitive pop anthem of the year.

Against this social backdrop, I had been happily getting on with my school life in Second Year at Howarth Cross High School on Albert Royds Street, Rochdale. The Labour Council's education

ECHOES OF '69

policy had been devoutly "Comprehensive" for at least three years but both pupils and teachers still felt like guinea pigs in some ghastly social experiment. Despite all egalitarian aspirations, my Year was "streamed" by perceived intellectual ability, and I was happy to be placed in the "top class", 2A1. Others, less fortunate, would find themselves in class 2C2 and cruelly referred to, by the teachers, as the "Remedial class". We were lucky, however, in that the school was housed in a brand new building (built on the site of my former Primary school, Halifax Road Juniors) and the facilities were superb and state-of-the-art. I fondly remember feeling very sophisticated and mature as, standing at the counter of the Tuck Shop in the second year Common Room, I bought Gillian Taylor a bottle of Strawberry Hubble Bubble and a Wagon Wheel (what a lady-killer, all four foot ten of me!). Coincidentally, outside Old Trafford last Saturday before the Premier League game against Sunderland, they were handing out Wagon Wheels as part of some promotion and I was struck by how small they seemed compared to my memory of them from 1968. The same applies to Cadbury's Crème Eggs. Is it me or does everyone think that things used to be bigger? I'll ask my wife!

One of my strongest memories from the first half of 1968 was the evening of 29th May - the occasion being Manchester United beating Benfica of Portugal 4-1 after extra time at Wembley to win the European Cup (as it was then known) for the first time. At this precise point in my short life, I would have enthusiastically described myself as a United fan, never anticipating the sea-change in my football affections that would impact within a little over two months. That night, however, I was every inch (all 58!) a Red and I remember weeping tears of joy as Bobby Charlton handed the elusive trophy to Matt Busby. I seem to recall that my dad was close to tears as well. Of course he'd reared me on tales of the Busby Babes and the Munich air disaster so, if anything, it probably meant even more to him.

At this time I was not a prolific football spectator. In fact, I was eight years old when I was taken to my first game - but what a

JULY 1968

game! The occasion was the Quarter-Finals of the European Cup-Winners' Cup, the first leg of the tie between Manchester United and Sporting Lisbon. This was, of course, a midweek evening game played under the Old Trafford floodlights and the most intense sensory experience of the author's young life (and in retrospect, probably a defining formative moment in my life). The match attracted a crowd of 60,297 and my Dad had got us tickets for what was then open terracing in the Scoreboard End. Being only knee-high to Gianfranco Zola (i.e. a midget) I didn't have a snowball in hell's chance of seeing any part of the game, but as kick-off time approached I was bodily picked up and passed from hand-to-hand over the heads of the crowd before being deposited on a ledge of the flat-roofed building which, I believe, housed the Groundsman's equipment. From this perch I enjoyed an unimpeded, and probably unrivalled, view of a fantastic game in which United eventually ran out 4-1 winners courtesy of a Denis Law hat-trick and another goal by Bobby Charlton. However, as all football supporters know from bitter experience, every silver lining has a cloud (!) and my young world was shattered two weeks later when my Dad gently broke the news to me that United had lost the return leg 5-0.

Over the next three years, I probably saw only a dozen games. Annual birthday treats of a trip to Old Trafford were punctuated by occasional trips to Spotland and, one snowy Saturday in January 1966, my dad took me to Maine Road. I suspect that he and my mum had had a disagreement and he took me simply to get out of the house - I can think of no other logical reason for going! The day sticks in my mind because City chose to turn out in a disgusting chocolate brown kit for better visibility on a snow-covered pitch - not the kind of thing to which a young child should be subjected!

The final week of the 1966/67 season was particularly memorable for me as a ten year old. On the 6th May, I somehow persuaded my parents to let me go to Spotland **on my own.** This was a major achievement in the total growing-up process, even if the ground was only three miles (but two separate buses) from

ECHOES OF '69

home. The first match I had attended unaccompanied (even if my dad, who was on duty that day, did take me home in a police car afterwards), and the occasion was only slightly marred by The Dale suffering an unfortunate 3-1 reversal to Wrexham (Jenkins scoring for the home team). However, the following week, the season was rounded off (if you'll forgive the expression!) when I was taken to Old Trafford to see Gordon Banks' arse! The gentle reader will appreciate that the purpose of the trip was not actually to see Gordon Banks' arse but in fact to see United play Stoke City and then be presented with the Championship trophy. My dad had us positioned at the Stretford End when the gates opened at 12:30 and we managed to get into the seats above the terracing. Banks' loudly-cheered exhibition came in response to the United fans taunting him with "We all agree, Stepney is better than Banks is, for Banksy is a no-good bum and so is Bonetti". Today we call it mooning; then it was unheard of. Then, everybody laughed and clapped and that was the end of it (sorry!): today, some sad character would register a complaint, or Sky would film it, and Banks would face a disrepute charge, probably ending up banned for three or more games. I guess the moral is, progress isn't everything it's cracked up to be!

Season 1967/68 was when John and I first started going to Spotland together. We went pretty regularly during the first half of the season but, for reasons which escape me, we did not see a single game after Christmas. Thinking about it more, it was probably that the team was crap! Eventually The Dale finished in nineteenth position in the old Fourth Division; a mere two points away from the dreaded "application for re-election" in those far-off days before automatic relegation to the Conference. I confess to not remembering too much about the few games we did see that season but there was one night game, possibly against Hartlepool United, when I recall the floodlights (partially) failing. Again, my dad was on duty that evening, and as an Inspector at that time, he was entitled to ponce around carrying a stick (don't ask!). In the gloomy confusion occasioned by the absence of floodlights (actually, given

JULY 1968

the state of Spotland's floodlights at that time it was a wonder anyone noticed they'd gone out) a number of kids came onto the pitch for a wander around. Later my Dad told me that, presumably as a prank, someone had aimed a kick at his behind in the dark - I think it was more likely a reaction to being given a crack with his stick as he tried to get them off the pitch (police brutality had not yet been discovered - it had existed for many years, but it hadn't been discovered. Nudge, Nudge! Wink, Wink!). The following day at school, I overheard one of the third years, a little weasel of a kid called Jimmy from the council estate off Albert Royds Street, regaling his mates with a tale of how he had "kicked a copper up the arse" at Spotland the night before. Sadly, for his playground credibility, no one believed him but I was incensed. This was MY Dad he was referring to! Revenge was mine two days later as, in a crowded corridor during a lesson changeover, I found myself almost directly behind the despised Jimmy and managed to boot him up the "derriere" (we were doing French by this time!) without him realising who had done it - my first (and probably only) pre-meditated act of football-related violence! I don't think I ever told my dad - it was a peculiarly personal satisfaction.

The long hot summer of 1968 rolled on (we always remember them as "long and hot", even if they were long and wet!). School broke up and six weeks of playing football and cricket morning, noon and night lay ahead. Days spent driving the neighbours to distraction as misdirected balls (of various sizes and colours) had to be retrieved from rhubarb patches or privet hedges. Traipsing to the Corner Shop, exhausted from running around in 70 degree heat, to experience the exquisite pleasure to be enjoyed from that first suck at a giant frozen Jubbly, Mambo or Calypso before, two hours later, frostbite and hypothermia set in with the ice still only half consumed. The rainy days that you spent horizontal on the floor, flicking Subbuteo players of variously-coloured teams as the summer championship unfolded. Then, always at weekends, taking various shards of plastic to your Granddad for repair, courtesy of his

ECHOES OF '69

"special formula glue", most damage having resulted from tantrum stampings from your younger sister. The peaceful tranquility of a weekday afternoon on Halifax Road, Hamer, suddenly shattered by an enraged but as-yet-unbroken schoolboy voice: "MUUUMMMM!! I'm going to brain that girl! She's only gone and stamped on Denis Law again!" Halcyon days!

The pop charts of this (still pre-Radio One) month contained an even more eclectic mixture of music styles than normal. Consider the following which reached Number 1; "Baby Come Back" by the Equals, a catchy reggae-type tune before reggae had actually been "discovered" in the UK; an American classic, "Mony, Mony", by Tommy James and the Shondelles; and finally, the Grandma's favourite, "I Pretend" by Des O'Connor (yes, the same one!). What an assortment!

And yet, unbeknownst to us at this time (although, if we had paid more attention to the Rochdale Observer, it might actually have been "beknownst" to us) the seeds of footballing success were even now being sown at Spotland and in pre-season training on Lenny Barn. Manager Bob Stokoe had retained only a handful of players from the previous inglorious season, among them stalwarts Jenkins, Butler, Rudd and Smith plus youngsters Melledew, Fletcher and Riley. In addition, goalkeeper Les Green had been transferred to Derby County for the considerable sum (by Dale standards) of £8,000. Diligently, over the course of the summer, Stokoe worked to persuade other seasoned campaigners to join the cause as names including Harker, Ryder, Parry, Whitehead, Ashworth, Leech and Radcliffe were auditioned for immortality in the pantheon that was Rochdale F.C. Let's just remind ourselves of the respective pedigrees of these worthies:

Chris **Harker**; signed from Grimsby Town, having kept goal for Bury for a number of seasons. He started his career with Newcastle United.

Derek **Ryder**; specialist left-back signed from Cardiff City, whose first professional club was Leeds United.

JULY 1968

Colin **Parry**; a six-foot central defender whose only previous club was his home-town Stockport County.

Norman **Whitehead**; skilful young right winger who had spent a year with Southport, having joined them after helping Skelmersdale United to the Final of the F.A. Amateur Cup in 1967.

Joe **Ashworth**; another big defender, signed from Southend United, who had previously played for Bradford, York and Bournemouth.

Vinny **Leech**; signed from near-neighbours Bury, having helped The Shakers gain promotion to Division 2 in season '67/68. A local lad by birth (Facit, Whitworth), he first signed professional for Blackburn Rovers before joining Bury on a free transfer in 1961.

Vince **Radcliffe**; a Manchester lad, signed from Peterborough United, who he joined from Portsmouth.

In addition, the young goalkeeper Matt **Tyrie** was signed from Burnley as cover for the experienced Harker.

Another very significant change for the coming season was announced in the Rochdale Observer on 6th July. The team's first strip was to revert to the style of Blue shirts with White shorts which had last been worn in season 1956/57. Then, they had changed to Black and White vertically-striped shirts before adopting White shirts with Black shorts in 1960/61.

So it was "all systems go" for the new season ahead; new colours (which had necessitated liberal applications of blue paint to be slapped all over Spotland by teams of earnest volunteer helpers); a partial re-building of the Main Stand (actually the Only Stand), which had collapsed the previous season; and a new senior playing squad whose full details were:

NAME	AGE	BIRTHPLACE	PREVIOUS CLUB
Ashworth Joe	27	Leeds	Southend United
Butler Dennis	24	Macclesfield	Bolton Wdrs
Fletcher Joe	22	Manchester	Amateur
Harker Chris	29	Whitley Bay	Grimsby Town
Jenkins Reg	29	Millbrook	Torquay United
Leech Vinny	27	Whitworth	Bury
Melledew Stevie	22	Rochdale	Amateur

ECHOES OF '69

Parry Colin	24	Stockport	Stockport County
Radcliffe Vince	24	Manchester	Peterborough United
Riley Hughie	20	Accrington	Amateur
Rudd Billy	27	Manchester	Grimsby Town
Ryder Derek	21	Leeds	Cardiff City
Smith Graham	22	Pudsey	Leeds United
Tyrie Matt	19	Bellshill	Burnley
Whitehead Norman	20	Liverpool	Southport

The original listing of the playing squad as displayed above, was published in the Rochdale Observer on 29th July but, erroneously gave "Big Reg's" age as thirty-one. It may well have been that this had ruffled a few Cornish feathers because the newspaper's midweek edition of 21st August contained an apology for the inaccuracy, under the headline "Statistician's Crime", by the football correspondent Geoff Whitworth (moral: nobody messes with Big Reg!).

Everything was in place and the actual playing season was about to kick off at last.

3.

AUGUST 1968

Football is an art more central to our culture than anything the Arts Council deigns to recognise.
Germaine Greer (1996)

Against the backdrop of the Papal encyclical from the Vatican which declared that any form of artificial birth control was contrary to the Divine will, the re-birth of Rochdale F.C. was imminent (and if you think that this is a contrived link, worse will follow!). The other earth-shaking political event of this month was the occupation of Czechoslovakia by troops from Russia and other Warsaw Pact countries which threatened to return the world to the fearful Cold War days of the early 60s. Civil War was still raging in Nigeria/Biafra which would ultimately lead to starvation for millions in the months to come.

Domestically, a gas explosion in a block of flats at Ronan Point in London caused the corner of the tower block to collapse like a pack of cards. Subsequently, the gas supply was turned off to eleven end flats in the recently-built Ashfield Valley deck-access development, pending investigation into the London incident.

Football-wise, the Dale were dealt an early blow for the new season ahead when the Football Association imposed a seven-day suspension on Stevie Melledew following three bookings at the end of the previous season. This was, of course, before the days when referees brandished yellow and red cards like semaphore signallers on amphetamines, and no doubt many Dale fans were totally unaware that Melledew had this disciplinary cloud hanging over him. The ban would come into effect from 5th August and Stevie would therefore miss the opening League game against Scunthorpe United. This obviously factored into manager Stokoe's thinking and Melledew was omitted from the side for both pre-season friendlies.

Friday 2nd August
OLDHAM ATHLETIC 2 ROCHDALE 1
(Friendly)

The traditional Rose Bowl pre-season curtain-raiser was played this season at Boundary Park (the venue alternated each year) and this was the first time (after seven previous years) that a game had been won by the hosts. The Dale lined up as follows:

Harker
Leech   Parry   Ashworth   Ryder
Lee (sub. Smith)   Rudd
Whitehead   Fletcher   Jenkins   Butler

(Steve Lee appeared on a trial basis. He was obviously found guilty as he never appeared again!)

As a first run-out for a side containing a number of new faces playing for the first time together, this was not a bad performance against higher-league opponents. Little did we know then that, come the season's end, the two clubs would by-pass each other travelling in opposite directions as the Latics were unfortunately relegated. A tight defensive display saw the sides turnaround nil-nil at half-time before Johnstone opened the scoring for Oldham. Five minutes from the end Rochdale grabbed a deserved equaliser when substitute **Smith** fired home from a Whitehead cross. However, in the deepening gloom, as Latics had not bothered to turn on their floodlights for this prestigious game (!), Johnstone netted again to give Oldham the trophy.

AUGUST 1968

This left just one further practice match in which to get the team ready for Saturday's big kick-off.

Monday 5th August
ALTRINCHAM 2 ROCHDALE 4
(Friendly)

For this game, Stokoe kept faith with the players who had finished the Oldham game. He would have been happy to see his team take a four-goal lead midway through the second half, before an element of complacency set in against a team who were then a force to be reckoned with in non-league circles. The line-up was:

Harker
Smith   Parry   Ashworth   Ryder
Leech   Rudd
Whitehead   Fletcher   Jenkins   Butler

(Goalscorers for the Dale were; Jenkins, Whitehead, Butler and Rudd)

We kids were still in the middle of our "big holidays" but looking forward to the first game of the season on the following Saturday. On the Monday before, which was traditionally "washing" day in our part of the world, we were taking a break from the usual football or cricket games by tear-arseing around the neighbourhood on our bikes. The area behind the terraced houses on Halifax Road, which adjoined the Flower of the Valley public house at Hamer (my family lived in the first police house next to the pub), was an unadopted road. This is council-speak for "no tarmac" or, in other words, a dirt track. To a 12 year old with an under-developed sense of danger, this was a perfect environment for pulling a rear-wheel skid and we were perfecting our techniques accordingly. I remember my partner in crime on this day was a ginger-haired lad called Chris Higginbottom, who stayed at his Grandma's on Dover Street during

ECHOES OF '69

the week as his parents both worked. (I always wondered what his first days at school were like - as others mastered writing their name, **J-A-N-E S-M-I-T-H or P-E-T-E-R B-R-O-W-N,** there he would be slogging through **C-H-R-I-S-T-O-P-H-E-R H-I-G-G-I-N-B-O-T-T-O-M!**). Anyway, it being Monday, our racetrack contained irresistible obstacles in the form of fully-laden washing lines, held aloft by wooden props, strung across from the back yards of the houses. We would career through the drying clothes at top speed, ducking down to avoid the washing line and pull a skid, no doubt sending up a shower of stones and dust onto the freshly-washed garments and bedding. In retrospect, it was an accident waiting to happen and, sure enough, on one lap yours truly forgot to duck down in time! Chris later said that it was reminiscent of a "Tom and Jerry" cartoon. As I hit the washing line with my Adam's apple, I seemed to stop in mid-air as my bike careered on without me. Then forces of gravity took over and, fortunately for me, instead of being decapitated, the weakest line of resistance gave in first and the hook holding the washing line was pulled out. Unfortunately, it was still attached to the wood into which it was screwed. Doubly unfortunate, the piece of wood in question was an old window frame and the neighbourhood tranquility was again rudely shattered, this time by the sound of breaking glass as old Mrs. Mottershead's kitchen window shot towards me! For the sake of preserving the reader's delicate sensibilities, I will draw a veil over the rest of the day by saying that the author had an early night, a thick ear and a bottom that glowed in the dark.

Despite a severe cash-flow problem resulting from reparations to old Mrs. Mottershead's window, and after a late fitness test on the rope burns to my neck, I called for John on Saturday lunchtime as we set off for Spotland. We had a set routine for each home game which involved stopping off at the Club Shop. For some inexplicable reason, this was located on Smith Street (between Broadwater youth club and the Yelloway coach depot) in the town centre and therefore miles from the football ground but, hey! What

AUGUST 1968

do I know about marketing? I'm an accountant. I recall that we bought our new blue and white scarves and off we went to run the rule over our new-look team, discussing en route the Observer report that Bob Stokoe had tried to sign John Regan from Crewe Alexandra. Evidently he had turned down a move to the Dale. Like all true football supporters we viewed his decision philosophically - it was his loss and he would probably have turned out to be crap anyway!

Saturday 10th August
ROCHDALE 3 SCUNTHORPE UNITED 2
(Division 4)

Attendance: 3,183   Referee: Mr. G. Hartley (Wakefield) H-T: 2-0

What a cracking start to the season and very favourable impressions made by each of the new boys. Curiously, numbers one to seven were all making their League debuts for Rochdale (can you imagine even having numbers one to seven actually playing today, given the squad-numbering system?). The complete line-up was:

Harker
Radcliffe   Parry   Ashworth   Ryder
Leech   Rudd
Whitehead   Fletcher   Jenkins   Butler
(Riley was an unused substitute)

Talking to an old boy on the terraces next to us before the game, he warned us to watch out for Scunthorpe's left winger Punton. Evidently, this bald old git had almost single-handedly beaten the Dale in the two-legged League Cup Final of 1962 when he played for Norwich - proof again, if needed, that loyal supporters possess a truly elephantine memory, especially when our own team has been wronged. Today, however, the first half was one-way traffic with

ECHOES OF '69

the Dale playing great attacking football in bright sunshine. The first goal of the season arrived after 30 minutes as **Butler** played a one-two with Leech before cracking in a 20-yard right-footer from the corner of the box as he cut in. Joy was unbounded as, in first half injury-time, "little Billy" Rudd was chopped down in the penalty area and **Jenkins** crashed home the resultant penalty.

Half-time, and cue the ritual of changing ends. By this I refer, of course, to the fans, not merely the teams, as Dale fans would perform an exodus from the Pearl Street end, through the Wilbutts Lane terrace and onto "the Sandy", the legendary Sandy Lane End. I had forgotten all about this nomadic tribal activity until, a couple of seasons ago, I took my son Greg to a Conference game at Stalybridge Celtic. It was New Year's Day and, unfathomably, there was no League programme that day, so we went in search of any kind of football match and found it in the form of a local "derby" against Northwich Victoria. The look on Greg's face (he would have been about six at the time) was a picture as every one of the (bumper) 1,004 spectators passed before us to get to the opposite ends. Sadly, this is another old footballing quirk that has been lost to us with the advent of all-seater stadiums or, at best, discreet terraces or stands (some with self-contained "vomitories" - where the hell do they get this word from? Why can't they just say "that bit behind the stand where you can buy a pint and have a pee"; sometimes even in separate areas!).

Back to the Scunthorpe game and the second half. Things got even better as Whitehead's corner kick was handled in the box by a Scunny defender and **Jenkins** sent the 'keeper the wrong way with his second penalty. (Until a couple of years ago this held the record for the most penalties I had seen in a single game until David Dunn's uncle (!) awarded Blackburn three against the Dale at Ewood Park in the Worthington Cup). However, it went "a bit pear-shaped" in the last twenty minutes as Scunthorpe scored twice. First, Harker was penalised for taking too many steps (another quirk

AUGUST 1968

long gone from the game) and Kerr smashed in a tap-back from the resulting indirect free-kick inside the area. Then Harker made a great save but the ball ran to Deere, who tapped home the rebound. Rochdale desperately clung on to the final whistle for a win they probably deserved on the overall balance of play.

One funny incident in this match has, for some reason, always stuck in my memory. One of the Scunthorpe half-backs, I think it was Lindsey, attempted to trap the ball on his chest with his arms bent double in front of him as some players do. However, he forgot to move his arms as the ball came down and it ended up nestling there, like a goalkeeper who had just collected a cross (as I write this it occurs to me that I've seen Gary Neville almost do the same thing on more than one occasion). Inevitably, the ref blew for handball at which someone in the crowd shouted "t'cricket season's done lad- we're playing soccer now!". Timing of the delivery is everything in these situations.

A final note on this game comes from the match programme, which indicated that Season Tickets were on sale at the following prices:

STAND	£7-10-0
	(i.e. seven pounds and ten shillings)
PADDOCK	£5-10-0
GROUND	£4-10-0
GROUND (Juniors)	£2-10-0
STAND (Old Age Pensioners)	£3-15-0

This is a far cry from the £530 I currently pay for my (single) season ticket at Old Trafford and, indeed, is less than the £13.00 cost of seats for Greg and I in the Family Stand at Spotland for one match today. How times change!

ECHOES OF '69

Top of the charts this week was "Fire" by the Crazy World of Arthur Brown. This was the guy who ponced around on Top of the Pops with what looked like flaming antlers on his head in some strange substance-influenced Dante's inferno of his own imagination (actually I was surprised when I researched this because I always associated this song with '65 or '66, don't know why). Again showing how varied our musical tastes were in those days, it was eventually knocked off the Number 1 spot by the Beach Boys' "Do It Again".

Rochdale's next game would take them to Workington for a League Cup game.

Wednesday 14th August
WORKINGTON 2 ROCHDALE 1
(League Cup)

Attendance: 2,958   Referee: Mr P. Partridge   H-T: 1-0

Stokoe decided to stick with a winning formula and so the team was again:

Harker
Radcliffe   Parry   Ashworth   Ryder
Leech   Rudd
Whitehead Fletcher Jenkins Butler

(Melledew as substitute replaced Fletcher after 68 minutes)

The Dale failed to reproduce the flowing football of the first hour on Saturday and, shortly after Whitehead had hit a post with a rasping drive, Tinnion put the home team ahead on 42 minutes with an angled drive. Substitute **Melledew** equalised in the 78th minute but Ogilvie won the match for Workington with a low drive in the 90th minute. The Rochdale Observer's correspondent had the good grace to admit that Workington probably deserved it.

AUGUST 1968

Saturday 17th August
COLCHESTER UNITED 0 ROCHDALE 0
(Division 4)

Attendance: 3,969 Referee: Mr. Reynolds (Swansea) H-T: 0-0

Another trip to a far-flung outpost of English League football saw the Dale travelling to Layer Road. Both opening league games had been against teams just relegated from Division 3 but, yet again, this was a solid, tight defensive performance. The match had a controversial moment; Jenkins "scored" from a direct free kick but the referee disallowed it and made him take the kick again because the Colchester defenders had not retreated the requisite 10 yards. In the second half, Butler's shot hit a post as the Dale searched in vain for the winner. The team lined up as follows:

Harker
Radcliffe   Parry   Ashworth   Ryder
Leech   Rudd
Whitehead   Melledew   Jenkins   Butler

(Fletcher as substitute replaced Whitehead after 68 minutes)

Saturday 24th August
ROCHDALE 1 EXETER CITY 1
(Division 4)

Attendance: 3,225 Referee: Mr. V. James (York) H-T: 0-0

The Corinthian spirit was all but dead in English football by 1968 as rampant professionalism prevailed. Nowhere was this better (worse?) exemplified than the Leeds United teams of 1965 onwards, under the tutelage of that master of dirty tricks and gamesmanship, Don Revie. Every single outfield player from 2 to

ECHOES OF '69

11 could "look after himself on the pitch" (this is a journalistic euphemism for being a Dirty Ba***rd). Tackles from behind, shirt-pulling and ankle-tapping were commonplace and, looking back, it really is a wonder that there were so few serious injuries. Even the Dale were not above resorting to tactics like this as the game against Exeter would show.

The team was unchanged from the Colchester match:

Harker
Radcliffe   Parry   Ashworth   Ryder
Leech   Rudd
Whitehead   Melledew   Jenkins   Butler
(Fletcher as substitute replaced Jenkins after 75 minutes)

A fairly uneventful game sprang to life early in the second half as Ashworth gave away a penalty by "carting" an Exeter forward who would otherwise have surely scored - the definitive "professional foul". Even as an otherwise naïve and not particularly worldly-wise twelve year old, I accepted, and perhaps even expected, my heroes to perform in this manner. Not so, apparently, the Rochdale Observer's reporter who solemnly reported Ashworth's foul as "…an inexplicable and out-of-character act". Bollocks! This was Rochdale in League Division 4, not Pegasus or Corinthian Casuals in the Amateur Cup. We were to see "Big Joe" "putting himself around" a lot more before the season ended. The Dale's blushes were eventually spared in the 71st minute when **Melledew** nipped in front of the 'keeper to prod in a loose ball for the equaliser. It hadn't been particularly inspiring but we were unbeaten with four points from three games as we trooped home after the game.

A snippet from that day's match programme will perhaps help to convey the innocence of the age; "At the Scunthorpe match (two weeks before) the Refreshment Bars had a good day, particularly with the orange juice. Sorry we had to disappoint so many of you, but we just didn't think we should have such brilliant weather;

AUGUST 1968

anyhow we have taken steps to prevent a reoccurrence of this, so please support our Refreshment bars". As Rochdalians would say, "Eeeh, that's reet quaint, i'nt it not?".

Monday 26th August
BRENTFORD 1 ROCHDALE 1
(Division 4)

Attendance: 9,140 Referee: Mr. C. Burtenshaw (Great Yarmouth) H-T: 1-0

A Bank Holiday trip to London today for the boys in Blue, an afternoon "drive" somewhere in the North-West for the author with his family. At this time we had a gleaming white Ford Consul Cortina Mark Two; my Dad's pride and joy. I know it gleamed because it was my job to wash the darn thing each Sunday morning. I know it was my dad's pride and joy because he would often wash it again after I'd already done it, before wax polishing the coachwork! A couple of year's later, this vehicle was the catalyst for a period of domestic strife as my Dad traded it (a "C reg") in for a similar model (but "B reg" with lower mileage). This was not the major issue, however, as my Mum evidently detested the Spearmint Green colour of the new car and was positively affronted by the car roof which had an electrostatically-applied black flock coating. Hands up anyone who remembers these? They were very popular at the time, but exposure to the elements over time caused the flock to fall off, inducing a form of "vehicular alopecia" which was not very attractive!

Onto the game and an unchanged starting XI, but a slightly more defensive outlook with Smith named as substitute.

Harker
Radcliffe Parry Ashworth Ryder
Leech Rudd
Whitehead Melledew Jenkins Butler
(Smith as substitute replaced Butler after 68 minutes)

ECHOES OF '69

BRENTFORD FOOTBALL CLUB

OFFICIAL PROGRAMME

Season 1968-69   Price 9d.

Football League Division IV
BRENTFORD v. ROCHDALE
Monday, 26th August, 1968
Kick-off 7.30 p.m.

Reproduced by kind permission of AEROFILMS LTD.
THE STADIUM, GRIFFIN PARK

Next Home Games

WEDNESDAY, 4th SEPTEMBER, 1968	SATURDAY, 7th SEPTEMBER, 1968
BRENTFORD v. HULL CITY	**BRENTFORD v. CHESTERFIELD**
Football League Cup 2nd Round	Football League Div. IV
Kick-off 7.30 p.m.	Kick-off 3.15 p.m.

AUGUST 1968

The Dale fell behind after only 16 minutes when Dearden scored with an angled drive and it was a backs-to-the-wall performance to keep the score down to one. Radcliffe was booked as Rochdale defended ever more desperately. However, after Rudd was moved out to the left wing following Butler's substitution, it was his cross which **Melledew** headed home for the equaliser in the 70th minute. They managed to hold out for the last twenty minutes to become the first team to take a point from Griffin Park that season and maintain their own unbeaten League start.

The Rochdale Observer this week featured two interesting articles. Firstly, it reported on a "mystery blaze" at the Alfred Street Headquarters of Rochdale Borough Police Force which had caused quite a bit of damage. I don't recall the incident personally, but an old colleague of my dad's, the then Inspector Arfon Jones (he was Welsh in case there should be any doubt in the reader's mind), was evidently put in charge of the salvage operation. Given the circumstances - when the alarm was first set off it was ignored by the officers present who believed it was a prank - I would have hoped that Rochdale's "other boys in blue" would have taken the opportunity to re-christen him Arson Jones! Surely too good an opening to miss? The second item to attract the attention of "the Ob" was an open-air exhibition of modern art staged in the Town Centre. It was entitled "Sculpture in the Street" and, for over a week, the good citizens of Rochdale could be seen scratching their heads in amazement or confusion as they attempted to negotiate an obstacle course of concrete lumps and metal tubing along the length of the Esplanade. The Observer quoted one of the townsfolk as saying that it "looked like a building site" - this, in my view, would have been one of the more charitable opinions expressed but then they did not know of the horror to come some years later in the hideous form of the bus station!

For the Dale, the month of August was rounded off with another away game, this time in the Potteries.

ECHOES OF '69

Saturday 31st August
PORT VALE 1 ROCHDALE 1
(Division 4)

Attendance: 4,153 Referee: Mr. M. Kerkhof (Bicester) H-T: 0-1

This latest game saw a change in tactics and formation as manager Stokoe looked to "beef-up" midfield with the re-positioning of Ashworth, allowing Smith a first start of the season effectively at Butler's expense. The new line-up was:

Harker

Radcliffe　　Parry　　Smith　　Ryder

Leech　　　Ashworth　　　Rudd

Whitehead　Melledew　Jenkins

(Butler as substitute replaced Whitehead after 83 minutes)

The Dale started this match in the dizzy heights of fifth position in the League (sceptics said they were so high they'd developed nose-bleeds) and the tactical changes looked to be paying dividends as they took the lead in the 38th minute. Ryder, from the left of course, flighted a ball into **Melledew's** path and he smashed a shot into the top left hand corner to maintain an impressive scoring run. However, the sequence of draws was to be maintained as Chapman forced an equaliser for the Valeites after 55 minutes. So, as the first month of the season drew to a close, the League table saw Rochdale in a reasonably satisfactory tenth position, just two points (and that was all you got for a win in those days) off the top spot.

AUGUST 1968

FOOTBALL LEAGUE DIVISION 4

	P	HOME W	D	L	F	A	AWAY W	D	L	F	A	Pts
Lincoln City	5	3	0	0	8	1	1	0	1	1	5	8
Darlington	5	1	1	0	5	0	1	2	0	3	2	7
Bradford City	5	2	0	0	4	1	0	3	0	4	4	7
Aldershot	5	1	0	1	2	3	2	1	0	5	2	7
Brentford	5	2	1	0	8	2	0	2	0	3	3	7
Wrexham	5	2	0	0	5	0	0	2	1	1	2	6
Halifax Town	5	1	0	1	3	1	2	0	1	5	3	6
Doncaster Rovers	4	1	1	0	5	4	1	1	0	3	2	6
Swansea Town	5	0	3	0	2	2	1	1	0	3	2	6
ROCHDALE	**5**	**1**	**1**	**0**	**4**	**3**	**0**	**3**	**0**	**2**	**2**	**6**
Chester	4	2	0	0	7	1	0	1	1	2	4	5
Chesterfield	5	2	1	0	6	2	0	0	2	1	5	5
Workington	5	0	1	1	1	2	1	2	0	1	0	5
York City	5	1	2	0	4	3	0	1	1	1	3	5
Exeter City	4	1	1	0	5	2	0	2	0	2	2	5
Newport County	5	1	2	0	4	1	0	0	2	0	4	4
Southend United	5	1	1	0	3	2	0	1	2	4	8	4
Scunthorpe United	5	0	2	0	3	3	1	0	2	9	7	4
Grimsby Town	5	1	0	2	4	3	0	1	1	0	2	3
Port Vale	4	1	1	0	2	1	0	0	2	2	6	3
Peterborough Utd	5	0	2	0	3	3	0	0	3	1	5	2
Notts County	5	0	1	2	3	6	0	1	1	1	6	2
Bradford PA	5	0	2	1	2	3	0	0	2	0	6	2
Colchester United	5	0	1	2	1	6	0	0	2	1	9	1

Nevertheless, we supporters could take satisfaction from the fact that this was, **officially** ('cos the Rochdale Observer said so!), Rochdale's best start to a season since 1929 (when the seventh game was the first in which the team tasted defeat). At least this provided some meagre crumb of comfort as we prepared for the dreaded return to school (Boo! Hiss!).

4.

SEPTEMBER 1968

If you are truly serious about preparing your child for the future, don't teach him to subtract - teach him to deduct.
Fran Lebowitz, *Social Studies*, 1981.

The long summer holidays were over and it was time to return to Howarth Cross but this time as a member of the Top Year; Year 3, the senior group in the school, and I was happy to find myself in class 3A1. There had been some "promotion and relegation" issues during the "close season" but I was apparently sufficiently high up the table not to be affected by it (although I don't think I was in any danger of qualifying for Europe either). Consequently, the bulk of my circle of friends stayed virtually intact. The school had a very good reputation in Rochdale, in large amount due to the strict but fair management of the Headmaster, Jack Kershaw, who (out of earshot) was known as "Jack the Whack" because of his propensity to administer corporal punishment. Fortunately, I never had cause to meet him under these circumstances but I came into contact with him almost every morning, having been press-ganged into a role assisting the school secretaries to administer the token system for each day's school dinners. Clearly, there was a price to pay for being good at Maths and trustworthy! There were actually two Maths teachers who took our group, Messrs. Mitchell and Cooper. Phil Mitchell, rather like his Eastenders namesake, was a sadistic tyrant. Still young, and with a lingering acne condition, he was naturally labelled "Pimple" and delighted in holding up your sideburns (in our case not whiskers but long hair at the temple) until you were

SEPTEMBER 1968

hopping about on tiptoes. Colin Cooper on, the other hand, was a mild-mannered, prematurely bald chap who quickly won, and kept, the respect of his pupils. He ran a Chess Club on Tuesday lunchtimes and taught me the game. I vividly remember him tying me in knots one day to the extent that he confused me so much that I tried to take one of my own pieces!

Top of the charts that first week back was "I've Gotta Get a Message to You" by the Bee Gees, but it was succeeded the following week by the Beatles' "Hey Jude" which soon became a Spotland anthem (mainly because the lyrics were so easily picked up) - "Naaah, nah nah nana nah nah, nana nah nah, Rochdale..." etc. The Dale's first match in September was at home to Peterborough United, who, as pre-season promotion favourites, had made a poor start to life back in Division Four. The Football Association had effectively relegated them the previous season by the calculated manoeuvre of the deduction of nineteen league points as a punishment for paying "illegal" bonuses.

Saturday 7th September
ROCHDALE 1 PETERBOROUGH UNITED 1
(Division 4)

Attendance: 4,834 Referee: Mr. J. Taylor (Wolverhampton) H-T: 1-0

I believe that this was the first match I had attended where I was conscious of the referee **before** the match started. Jack Taylor was renowned as England's best ref and his officiating at Spotland was considered to be something of an event. I remember concentrating on his performance almost as much as that of my team and being favourably impressed. Bob Stokoe abandoned the experiment of playing Ashworth in midfield after just one game but the outcome of the match was the same - a 1-1 draw with **Melledew** scoring. This was becoming rather repetitive!

ECHOES OF '69

The line-up, back in 4-2-4 formation, was:

Harker

Radcliffe   Parry   Ashworth   Ryder

Leech   Rudd

Whitehead   Melledew   Jenkins   Butler

(Fletcher as substitute replaced Butler after 79 minutes)

Melledew opened the scoring for the Dale after 44 minutes but, marvellous as his scoring run was, it exposed a worrying trend in the Rochdale side, namely that no-one else looked remotely likely to score! This was most evident in the first 15 minutes after half-time when the Dale paralysed their opponents with great attacking football, but were unable to add to their goal advantage. The inevitable then happened. The "Posh" equalised through Hall in the 64th minute and indeed had chances to win before the final whistle. This view was obviously shared by the Rochdale Observer's Geoff Whitworth, who penned the following bizarre sentence as part of his match report; *"In the fifteen minutes immediately after the interval, Rochdale's control was such that Peterborough, unable to halt the non-stop assault, made the Battle of the Alamo look like victory for the Texans."* Wow! I'm sure he knew what he meant but I'm buggered if I do!

This match also saw me benefiting from a piece of outrageous good fortune. As usual, John and I had arrived at the ground pretty early, around 2:15 or so, and taken up our habitual pre-match position near the corner flag at the Pearl Street/Main Stand Paddock (if the weather was decent you could sit on the grass on the big hill that used to be there; in fact, I later fell asleep there during a particularly tedious pre-season friendly against Clydebank in August 1972). Anyway, a photographer came along and mustered all twelve or so of the people on the Ground at that time to bunch up together to make a "crowd scene" for his photograph. He told us to look in that evening's Football Pink and anyone whose head was

SEPTEMBER 1968

circled would win a Guinea (which was 21 shillings or £1.05 today). Crossing over Halifax Road to Howarth's Newsagents for a Football Pink was a Saturday evening ritual and I could set my watch by the yellow Manchester Evening News delivery van arriving at 5.55pm. Sure enough, as I sat there nervously waiting, fingernails bitten to the quick, the delivery was late. Twenty minutes later the van pulled up and the pink bundle was hurled into the shop doorway. I paid for my copy and hurriedly turned over the pages looking for the photo; there it was, and my head was ringed! I was mightily chuffed. Not only was this the first thing I had won since "Uncle Peter Webster's Talent Contest" on Blackpool's Central Pier as a four year old in 1960 (singing "My Old Man's a Dustman" in very strident tones, if you must know) but also the cash was a significant amount for a twelve year old in 1968, especially one whose piggy-bank was still depleted after the bike and washing-line incident. I had to present myself at the Evening News' Rochdale office, at the top of Drake Street, to prove my identity so my Dad drove me there on the Monday evening. I suggested that we go up to Hollingworth Lake first so that I could "borrow" one of the lifebelts and then stick my head through it before going into the "Pink" office, so that I would resemble the photo even more! My Dad, being a pillar of the local society and an educated man, told me I was a daft pillock.

Rochdale now faced the prospect of two tough away fixtures in the space of four days with trips to Chesterfield and Doncaster Rovers.

Saturday 14th September
CHESTERFIELD 1 ROCHDALE 1
(Division 4)

Attendance: 5,983 Referee: Mr. J. Thacker (Scarborough) H-T: 0-0

Quite incredibly, this was yet another 1-1 draw (establishing a record which stands to this day of the club's longest sequence of

ECHOES OF '69

League draws, six) with **Melledew** again notching Rochdale's solitary goal. The team had a familiar look to it but Fletcher, who had bagged a number of goals the previous season, was brought into the right side of the attack supposedly to provide more firepower. The full line-up was as follows:

Harker
Radcliffe   Parry   Ashworth   Ryder
Leech   Rudd
Fletcher Melledew Jenkins Butler

(Whitehead as substitute replaced Jenkins after 71 minutes)

Melledew was again the game's pivotal figure, but initially for all the wrong reasons. After a fairly dour first half, a disastrously misplaced backpass by Melledew in the 60th minute let in Hollet for the Spireites to open the scoring. To their credit, the Dale continued to battle, creating a number of good chances before, on 87 minutes, that man **Melledew** was again the team's saviour as his forehead arced the ball into the far corner for a deserved equaliser.

This result left Rochdale in tenth position in the League, now three points behind unbeaten leaders Darlington who had eleven points from their seven games. Next opponents, Doncaster Rovers, were handily placed in third with ten points and Stokoe, conscious that they had already bagged fourteen goals in the League, again tinkered with his side. Teenager Hughen Riley came in for his first start of the season on the right side of a three man midfield, with Jenkins, who had not yet scored from open play this season, dropping down to the bench.

SEPTEMBER 1968

Doncaster Rovers Football Club

OFFICIAL PROGRAMME

Tuesday, 17th September, 1968

Doncaster Rovers
versus
Rochdale

FOOTBALL LEAGUE — DIVISION IV

PRICE NINEPENCE
(including Football League Review)

ECHOES OF '69

Tuesday 17th September
DONCASTER ROVERS 2 ROCHDALE 0
(Division 4)

Attendance: 12,193 Referee: Mr. N. Graham (Newbiggin-by-the-sea) H-T: 0-0

Harker
Radcliffe   Parry   Ashworth   Ryder
Riley   Leech   Rudd
Fletcher   Melledew   Butler
(Jenkins was not used as substitute)

In front of a huge crowd, swollen by hundreds who travelled from Rochdale, Johnson opened the scoring for Rovers after 54 minutes and, despite lots of pressure from Rochdale, they could not force an equaliser. Gilfillian scored a second, on the break, in the last minute and Stokoe said that, whilst he was disappointed with the result, he was pleased with the team effort. The Dale's programme for the next game summed up this match as follows: *"Tuesday's game was an exciting, interesting and close affair. We had the better of the first half and had Doncaster supporters readily admitting that we were the best side the Rovers had met this season. A goal to Doncaster just after the interval gave them greater confidence, but we came back with a fighting show and could have claimed the equaliser. Doncaster's second goal in the closing minute made the final score an injustice."* Reasonable, impartial and balanced, if you ask me! However, the result saw Rochdale drop a place to eleventh in the table.

Elsewhere, in the world at large, the month of September saw thousands killed as a result of earthquakes in Iran, the two-tier postal system was introduced in the UK (5d for first class, 4d for second) and the major banks announced that, from July 1969, they would close on Saturdays. Soviet tanks left Prague but strict censorship of press, TV and radio was imposed by the Politburo

SEPTEMBER 1968

puppet-master who was "advising" the Czech government. Full frontal nudity was seen on the London stage in "Hair" and the South African government cancelled the winter cricket tour by the M.C.C. after Basil d'Oliveira was included in the touring party. I took the opportunity to ask my wife Lynn, who is four years older than me, if she remembered any of these events. She replied that the only thing that she recalled from 1968 was that she wore mini-skirts so short that you could see her knickers if she bent over more than an inch! Mind you, this is from the woman whose answer to the question, on "Who Wants To Be A Millionaire?", "…with which band do you associate the names Robert Plant and Jimmy Page?" jumped in, before the four possible answers came up, with "Emerson, Lake & Palmer"!

Back on the football front, the club moved quickly in response to the first defeat of the season by signing centre-forward (that's a striker for anyone under 25!) Terry Melling from Third Division side Mansfield Town for the hefty sum of £2,000. Yes, the same silver-tongued Melling who I mentioned in my introduction and who had (probably) also verbally abused spectators at his other clubs Newcastle United, Watford and Newport County! At school, the playground consensus was that this was a good move and a sign that the club had serious ambitions. Then the playground went back to swapping "Footballer" or "American Civil War" bubblegum cards (I don't recall which were "in" that autumn but I seem to remember that they were made by "A.B.&C. cards and gum"? If anyone knows drop me an e-mail). For the Dale fans among our number, Saturday's game with Bradford City could not come quickly enough.

ECHOES OF '69

Saturday 21st September
ROCHDALE 6 (SIX!) BRADFORD CITY 0
(Division 4)

Attendance: 4,118 Referee: Mr. K. Burns (Dudley) H-T: 3-0

What a complete and unmitigated disaster! You might expect that I would have been cock-a-hoop (sorry! In proper football-speak, "over the moon") after a result like this but I wasn't, for the simple reason that **I MISSED THE MATCH!!!** This was the first in what would become a highly-disturbing sequence in which, quite simply, there was a pre-ordained pattern - if I failed to attend a game, Rochdale would score a sh**-load of goals! On the day of this match, there was a deluge of Biblical proportions which reached a crescendo just after lunch (my guinea pig was frantically looking for a partner to keep him company in the Ark, it was so bad!). Undeterred, I put on my (still-pristine) blue and white scarf in preparation for setting forth when I heard the dreaded parental words which chilled my young heart; "You're not going to a football match in this weather! You can come to your Grandma and Grandad's with us". Oh misery! Despite my increasingly animated protests (suicide or running away with the circus might have been mentioned during the discussion) the die was cast, the decision absolutely final. I found myself in the car travelling **up** Halifax Road towards Littleborough instead of **down** towards the Town Centre. After being encouraged to say a word to my grandparents on arrival (I think the word they eventually got was "hello"), I settled down in a morose and dejected fashion to watch "Grandstand" or "World of Sport", probably both. What a way to spend a Saturday afternoon when you know that your team are playing at home not five miles away! Sat there listening to the inane blatherings of David Coleman/Frank Bough or (worse still) Dickie Davies (was anyone ever more appropriately named?). Instead of watching my heroes in Blue and White, I had to endure a diet of horse-racing from Uttoxeter, swimming from Crystal Palace and

SEPTEMBER 1968

Rugby League from Headingley (Eddie Waring commentating on 'Ull Kingston Rrrrovers having an "up 'n' under" against 'Unslet; I wished he'd had "an early bath"). Finally the ultimate in squirm-inducing horror. An hour spent biting your nails waiting for the Final Scores at five o'clock whilst Kent Walton described Mick McManus' choreographed attempts to get a knockout (or two falls or two submissions) against Jackie Pallo, Billy Two Rivers, Les Kellett or Bert Royal, all set against the backdrop of your Gran intermittently shouting "oooh yer dirty bugger!". So-called "Professional Wrestling"! Welcome grapple fans! Bog off Kent (I think I said Kent). To make matters worse, as we were watching ITV, I didn't even get an early release from my misery in the form of the Teleprinter results service as they came in. No, I had to squirm my way through all the results from Divisions One, Two and Three before, finally, there it was in black and white before me; Rochdale 6 Bradford City 0! I didn't know whether to laugh or cry! Words didn't fail me. I just kept them to myself, conscious of the fact that, in this very room two years previously, I had been "sent off" to the kitchen and temporarily "excluded" for the first five minutes of extra time of the World Cup Final for shouting "BAST**DS" at the bloody Germans when Weber equalised in the last minute of normal time against England. What a confusion of emotions! Joy that my team had triumphed so comprehensively; despair that they could ever have done so without my support. I recall the wise words of my Gran; "You'd be better off not going to any more matches, they might get promoted!" Words in jest but could it be true? Was it conceivable that I was a Jonah, a jinx on my team? Surely not? But, when you are just twelve, you have to consider such possibilities and I worried over it for the rest of the weekend before rationalising that this was a simple one-off, never to be repeated occurrence that I would laugh about when I was older. Little did I know!

ECHOES OF '69

For the record, the team line-up, in its new 4-3-3 formation to accommodate Melling, was this:

Harker
Radcliffe   Parry   Ashworth   Ryder
Leech   Rudd   Butler
Fletcher   Melledew   Melling
(Riley was not used as substitute)

As neither of us were on the phone at home, I'd had no way of letting John know that I was not going to the match but apparently his Mum wouldn't let him go either (although he was convinced that, if I'd called for him, she would have done). We consoled each other on Monday back at school and listened to one of the other lads describe the momentous events of what, evidently, was the Dale's best result since 1949(!) when they had beaten Mansfield by the score of 7-1.

GOAL No 1; after 23 minutes, **Butler** slipped the ball wide of the keeper.

GOAL No 2; in the 30th minute, **Rudd** volleys home from 6 yards after Melledew's clever back-heel flick.

GOAL No 3; four minutes later, **Melledew** swivels and hooks in Radcliffes's cross from the by-line.

GOAL No 4; with 69 minutes gone, **Fletcher** fires home after running on to Melling's through pass.

GOAL No 5; Melledew taps in his second from a quick centre after 74 minutes.

GOAL No 6; Two minutes from the end, **Fletcher** rounds off the scoring with his second as, on the goal line, he forces home Melledew's centre.

Melling failed to get on the score sheet himself, but he had played a pivotal role in Rochdale producing their best performance of the season to date, the Board getting an immediate return on their investment. The result took the Dale up to eighth place in the table with ten points from their nine

SEPTEMBER 1968

games, now just four points behind joint leaders Darlington and Doncaster Rovers.

Our next game would be away to York City, who were on the crest of a slump following successive stuffings away to Port Vale (0-3) and Brentford (1-5). The day was also my sister Lindsay's seventh birthday and, resplendent in her new Bizzy Lizzy dress with the magic pocket (surely you've not forgotten this Watch with Mother classic?; you must remember her curious Eskimo companion Little Mo? No, not the one from EastEnders), she had a party at home. Since the start of term at Smallbridge Junior school (the old Halifax Road Juniors renamed when the new school was built on Buckley Road) we had continually heard about "our kid's" best friend, the seemingly ostentatiously named Pamela Whitcombe-Jane. You tended to find few double-barrelled names in our neck of the woods and consequently, when she arrived, I did my best big brother bit and greeted our guest with "Welcome Miss Whitcombe-Jane". Her reply, "Why are you calling me that? My name's Pamela Jane Whitcombe" would not be the last time that my younger sister would contrive to make me look an even bigger prat than I really was!

Saturday 28th September
YORK CITY 0 ROCHDALE 0
(Division 4)

Attendance: 3,364   Referee: Mr. J. Quinn (Middlesbrough) H-T: 0-0 (patently)

Following the old adage, "why change a winning side?", Bob Stokoe named the same team which had demolished Bradford City.

Harker
Radcliffe   Parry   Ashworth   Ryder
Leech   Rudd   Butler
Fletcher   Melledew   Melling
(Whitehead was not used as substitute)

ECHOES OF '69

However, from a goalscoring perspective, it was a case of "feast to famine" as, by all accounts, York's goalkeeper Widdowson played a blinder and withstood everything Rochdale could throw at him. The Dale defence, on the other hand, was largely untroubled throughout the game and, in the end, the single point gained was a disappointment. As a result, Rochdale dropped a place to ninth in the table and were now five points behind the leaders and three points off a promotion spot.

Commendably, the Club's Fighting Fund Committee provided transport to the match, and a free meal afterwards, as a "thank you" for all the volunteers who had helped with the repairs and re-painting operation during the summer.

Mary Hopkins' chart-topping song at the end of September summed it up perfectly:

Those were the days, my friend,
We thought they'd never end.

SEPTEMBER 1968

The League table looked like this as September drew to a close:

FOOTBALL LEAGUE DIVISION 4

	P	HOME W	D	L	F	A	AWAY W	D	L	F	A	Pts
Darlington	10	4	1	0	11	2	2	3	0	7	2	16
Doncaster Rovers	10	4	1	0	11	5	3	1	1	7	4	16
Chester	10	5	1	0	15	4	1	2	1	6	7	15
Lincoln City	10	4	0	1	11	2	2	2	1	4	7	14
Aldershot	10	2	1	2	4	5	4	1	0	11	5	14
Swansea Town	10	1	4	0	5	4	3	1	1	8	4	13
Brentford	10	4	1	0	14	3	0	3	2	6	10	12
Bradford City	10	3	1	0	8	2	1	3	2	7	13	12
ROCHDALE	**10**	**2**	**2**	**0**	**11**	**4**	**0**	**5**	**1**	**3**	**5**	**11**
Workington	10	1	3	1	6	5	2	2	1	2	1	11
Newport County	10	3	2	1	11	6	1	0	3	6	8	10
Southend United	10	3	1	0	5	2	0	3	3	7	12	10
Halifax Town	10	2	0	2	5	5	2	1	3	6	7	9
Colchester United	10	2	1	2	3	6	1	2	2	5	11	9
Wrexham	10	3	0	1	8	3	0	2	4	1	6	8
Scunthorpe Utd	10	2	2	0	6	4	1	0	5	13	16	8
York City	10	2	3	0	6	4	0	1	4	2	12	8
Exeter City	10	1	3	1	10	8	0	2	3	5	9	7
Port Vale	9	3	1	1	9	4	0	0	4	2	9	7
Peterborough Utd	10	2	2	1	9	8	0	1	4	2	7	7
Grimsby Town	10	2	1	3	6	5	0	2	2	1	6	7
Chesterfield	10	2	2	2	7	6	0	0	4	1	8	6
Bradford PA	11	1	4	2	7	11	0	0	4	1	11	6
Notts County	10	1	1	3	6	10	0	1	4	5	14	4

5.

OCTOBER 1968

The natural state of the football fan is bitter disappointment, no matter what the score.
Nick Hornby, *Fever Pitch* (1992)

Printer's deadlines for football programmes often lead to editorial comments being overtaken by unforeseen events and this was never more so than in the Rochdale match programme for 5th October. The Club Notes page carried this opening paragraph:

"Recently, high in the pop record charts was the song "Wonderful World" (sung by Louis Armstrong). Here at Spotland it's the club's unofficial signature tune at the present time. The clouds are at last showing the long looked for silver lining. Every other similar cliché springs to mind. It is not, we believe, a case of our being over optimistic and cheering prematurely. In fact, given a little luck, and particularly if we can keep a fit staff, then there is good reason to believe the wonderful world will look better still in a month's time".
Everything in the garden was rosy then? Well no actually, it was not! What the editor wasn't aware of was the previous day's development that would provoke banner headlines of

SOCCER CLUB BOMBSHELL!

as news broke of Bob Stokoe's decision to leave Rochdale to take up the manager's position at Second Division Carlisle United. The Rochdale Board issued a statement that they had "reluctantly agreed to Bob Stokoe's acceptance of the Carlisle job". In fact, they had no

OCTOBER 1968

choice. Stokoe apparently was not under contract with the Club and believed that he had a "gentleman's agreement" to talk to **any** club from a higher level which might approach him. He rejected every inducement made to him to stay, saying that he wanted to prove himself in a higher level of football (and he subsequently did just that in May 1973 when he managed Second Division Sunderland to a fairy tale F.A. Cup Final victory over Leeds United). Dale Chairman Fred Ratcliffe was critical of the manner in which Carlisle had gone about the matter, in terms of approaching Stokoe directly rather than through the Club, but the Board wasted no time in appointing Len Richley as his successor. Richley's message to the fans was simple; "Let's get on with the job!".

Saturday 5th October
ROCHDALE 0 WORKINGTON 0
(Division 4)

Attendance: 4,584 Referee: Mr. D. Turner (Rugeley, Staffs) H-T: 0-0

Harker
Radcliffe   Parry   Ashworth   Ryder
Leech   Rudd   Butler
Fletcher   Melledew   Melling

(Jenkins as substitute replaced Fletcher after 62 minutes)

A decent sized crowd turned out for a match featuring two of the meanest defences in the Division and it should have been no surprise that the respective goalkeepers remained unbeaten throughout the ninety minutes. Writing in the Rochdale Observer, correspondent Derek Nicholls was clearly struggling to fill his allotted space with a match report, such was the paucity of action and good football. He was, however, deeply troubled by what he deemed Richley's inheritance when he penned the following, almost completely unintelligible, opening paragraph:

ECHOES OF '69

Some fortunes are bequeathed with strings and the string attached at Spotland was sufficiently problematic at what might be termed the reading of the will to give even the inheritance a hand-me-down look. WHAT?

He went on to report that "Whether through inaccuracy or intent, a veritable stream of (Rochdale) crosses terminated at the near post" and finished his report, with almost religious fervour, with the final sentence: "Let us all give thanks for the sheer dominance of Parry, in the air and on the ground, in an unflustered personal display which, as well as averting embarrassment for individual colleagues now and then, may well have saved Rochdale one point". PHEW! You know what they say about the Sixties; "If you can remember them, you weren't there", but what was this guy on? As a Dale supporter, you had to have a pretty good level of education simply to understand the match reports, it seemed.

The same weekend saw a unique sporting moment as, in the United States Formula One Grand Prix, British drivers finished first, second and third. Respectively, they were, Jackie Stewart (who I would get to meet a couple of years later when he brought his Tyrell car for a promotion at Tom Mellor Ford on Oldham Road), Graham Hill and John Surtees.

Monday 7th October
ROCHDALE 0 BRENTFORD 0
(Division 4)

Attendance: 4,958 Referee: Mr. K. Styles (Barnsley) H-T: (wait for it!) 0-0

I didn't go to this match as I had not yet convinced my parents that twelve year olds could stay out until ten o'clock on school nights (hey come on! - I was still trying to get them to let me out in the rain!). However, on this occasion, I didn't miss very much as a rather dreary draw was played out before what was, for a Monday

OCTOBER 1968

night game versus London opposition, a pretty decent crowd. As the Observer poetically commented, *"The terrace weeds are at last being trampled back into the concrete"!* Brentford were, by all accounts, a very physical side and had two players booked on the night. Whitehead replaced Fletcher as the formation reverted to a more flexible 4-2-4 under Manager Ritchley.

Harker
Radcliffe   Parry   Ashworth   Ryder
Leech   Rudd
Whitehead   Melledew   Melling   Butler
(Jenkins was an unused substitute)

The result took the Dale to the dizzy heights of seventh place in the table as they prepared to take on leaders Darlington at Feethams in their next game.

Saturday 12th October
DARLINGTON 0 ROCHDALE 0
(Division 4)

Attendance: 7,113   Referee: Mr. B. Daniels (Rainham, Essex)   H-T: 0-0

Injuries to Radcliffe (thigh) and Melledew (ankle) brought enforced changes to the side.

Harker
Smith   Parry   Ashworth   Ryder
Leech   Rudd
Whitehead   Jenkins   Melling   Butler
(Riley was an unused substitute)

On the positive side, this was the first time that Darlington had failed to score this season and it was Harker's fifth consecutive

ECHOES OF '69

clean sheet. On the other hand, the Dale couldn't even buy a goal during this period. Darlington had just had an excellent win at Doncaster (before an amazing 22,000 crowd) and Tyne-Tees TV filmed the game for Sunday afternoon highlights. Granada TV's Gerald Sinstadt was, for the time, a reasonable commentator/presenter but how nice it would have been to hear someone telling it like it really was; a Ron Atkinson type figure who would have said that Rochdale's forward line "couldn't hit a cow's arse with a banjo!". The Dale mainly played a long-ball game; Melling had a couple of shots saved and Jenkins shaved a post with another, but again it was a dour performance.

This weekend also saw the opening of the 1968 Olympic Games in Mexico. They would throw up British heroes as David Hemery (in the 400 metres hurdles) and Chris Finnegan (the Middleweight boxer) both picked up Gold medals. Lillian Board collected Silver in the 400 metres but, tragically, would die of cancer only two years later. The Games would be best remembered, however, for three remarkable incidents. In the first, the American high jumper, Dick Fosbury, staggered the millions watching on TV as he abandoned the traditional straddle jump technique and approached the bar from an acute angle before turning backwards and clearing the bar head first - the eponymous "Fosbury Flop". Next, the Games were hijacked politically as two Black American athletes, Tommy Smith and John Carlos, shocked the world by raising gloved hands at their medal ceremony in support of the nascent "Black Power" movement. Finally, in an epoch-defining moment, the American long jumper, Bob Beamon, stunned everyone when he shattered the world record with an incredible leap. In the Maths department at Howarth Cross, we marked the length of the jump in red masking tape along the floor of the corridor and marvelled at the achievement; 8.90 metres, more than half a metre farther than the previous world record, and one that would last until 1991.

OCTOBER 1968

Saturday 19th October
ROCHDALE 0 SWANSEA TOWN 1
(Division 4)

Attendance: 4,889 Referee: Mr. W. Handley (Cannock, Staffs.) H-T: 0-0

Harker

Radcliffe   Parry   Ashworth   Ryder

Leech   Rudd

Whitehead   Melledew   Melling   Butler

(Jenkins as substitute replaced Ashworth after 26 minutes)

The Dale game plan was totally disrupted after 26 minutes when Ashworth limped off with a leg injury. Leech was forced to drop back into the back four with Melledew taking his position in midfield, thereby accommodating sub Jenkins up front. Rochdale had the better of this first half but again suffered from wayward shooting. They literally paid the penalty in the second half. Harker failed to cut out a cross and Radcliffe was adjudged to have used his arm in clearing the resultant shot off the line. Gwyther easily converted the spot-kick to hand Swansea the victory, although Melledew hit the bar in the last minute.

 There was a humorous incident during the match which continued to amuse John and I as we walked home and helped to take our minds off the disappointment of the result. An old boy in a flat cap (I know I said I wouldn't mention these but this is factual reporting - he was wearing one!) had decided, mid-way through the first half, that he was far from satisfied with the effort, commitment and contribution from Rochdale's right winger, Norman Whitehead. Each time the hapless Whitehead got the ball (and subsequently lost it) old flat cap would shout out what, in the Queen's English, would have been "..half-hearted". However, this is not an expression which translates well in "Lanky" dialect and the resultant "..arf'arted" was a gift to two giggling twelve year olds who were convinced that he was shouting a personal

ECHOES OF '69

confession of his own incipient flatulence! The subject of Lancashire dialectic expressions that I've heard at football matches could form the contents of a book in its own right but, for the sake of brevity, I will list a few personal favourites with appropriate translation (please bear in mind that one of the key attributes of "Lanky" is that you string all the words in a sentence together without break in their delivery!):

"*Gerrim gelded*" - "*drastic measures are required to stop their winger who is tormenting our full-back*"

"*Tha's a nose lahk a blind cobbler's thumb*" - "*Your nose is an odd shape*"

"*That's pissed on't chips*" - "*What an unfortunate goal to concede*"

"*Tha favvers tha's seen thi own arse*" - "*Cheer up old chap*"

"'*Ee cud'nt stop a pig in a ginnel*" - "*Their centre-forward is a tad bow-legged*"

"*Tha's a face like a well slapped arse*" - "*Sir, you have a ruddy complexion*"
"*He's lahk a dog wi' two dicks*" - "*He is quite pleased with life*"

"*Tha's as much use as a chocolate fireguard*" - "*Your contribution to the team is negligible*"

"*Oooh, reet in't wedding tackle*" - "*The ball has unfortunately struck his private parts*"

All the above were genuinely heard at Spotland, but my all-time favourite piece of "Lanky Lingo" (and, obviously, not heard at a match) is the pithy **"Astibinmenbinmam"** - "Tell me mother, have the refuse collectors called yet". Beautiful!

OCTOBER 1968

The defeat by Swansea, in which Rochdale lost their unbeaten home record, had seen the Dale fall to a rather dismal thirteenth position in the league, and the injury to Joe Ashworth had seen Len Richley experiment with Jenkins in a centre-back role in the midweek Lancashire Senior Cup game. The match, against neighbours Oldham Athletic, ended one-all with Melledew again on target.

Hooliganism and violence made their first recorded appearance at Spotland during this season. At the Bradford City game, there had been some jostling between rival fans during the half-time change of ends and objects were thrown onto the pitch during the second half. The club was warned by the Football League as to its future conduct and required to post warning notices at the ground and in the match programme. Perversely, this happened at precisely the same time that the Club received a "John White fair play award" for the fans behaviour and support during August. However, there was a serious incident during the Oldham game when a seventeen year old lad from Oldham had to be stretchered off the terrace at half-time with a head injury, allegedly having been struck with a bottle.

For the next league game, however, Graham Smith replaced Ashworth as the Dale made the long journey to Essex to face a Southend United team now two places above them in the table.

Saturday 26th October
SOUTHEND UNITED 1 ROCHDALE 3
(Division 4)

Attendance: 9,346 Referee: Mr. T. Reynolds (Swansea) H-T: 0-0

Harker
Radcliffe   Parry   Smith   Ryder
Leech   Rudd
Whitehead   Melledew   Melling   Butler

(Jenkins was an unused substitute)

ECHOES OF '69

Parry was back, having missed the Oldham game with injury, but Ashworth was still out, Smith deputising. It looked like the usual story as the Dale defended stoutly, but they were rocked by conceding a goal after 72 minutes as Best scored for the home side. However, the fighting spirit in the side was there for all to see as Rochdale hit back almost immediately as a Ryder free-kick was headed down by Melling to Butler. **Butler** nutmegged the defender before lashing the ball past the 'keeper. Then, on 82 minutes, from a Whitehead pull-back, **Butler** was on hand again to hook the ball home. Victory was completed in the last minute as **Melledew** threw himself horizontally to meet Melling's centre and head the ball in. What a comeback!

As October drew to a close, Mary Hopkin's "Those Were the Days" remained at Number 1 in the charts, a position she had occupied all month as rumours grew that her mentor, one Paul McCartney no less, was taking more than a professional interest in her development. Paul's song-writing partner, John Lennon, was busted for drug possession and appeared in his first film ("How I Won The War") and Enoch Powell M.P. was increasingly vocal in his opposition both to immigration and to the Race Relations Bill, which received Royal Assent this month. At school, half-term approached as our juvenile sense of humour gathered pace. A series of jokes each beginning "..meanwhile back at the ranch" was doing the rounds. My particular favourite, as I recall, was - "..meanwhile back at the ranch, Tonto, not knowing that the Lone Ranger was disguised as a door, shot his knob off!"

The Dale had another go at beating Oldham in the Lancashire Cup on the evening of Monday 28th, but the match again ended in a draw. **Melledew** and a **Hunter o.g.** registered for Rochdale and even extra time could not separate the teams. Captain Rudd at least won the coin toss to determine home advantage in the second replay. The victory at Southend had re-ignited Dale supporters' hopes that the team might achieve something this season as they closed the month in eleventh place, six points behind the leaders but

OCTOBER 1968

only four off the last promotion spot. This is how the complete table looked as the month ended.

FOOTBALL LEAGUE DIVISION 4
October 31, 1968

	P	HOME W	D	L	F	A	AWAY W	D	L	F	A	Pts
Darlington	15	5	2	1	13	4	3	4	0	8	2	22
Chester	15	7	1	0	21	5	1	4	2	10	12	21
Aldershot	15	5	1	2	13	9	4	2	1	12	8	21
Doncaster Rovers	15	6	1	1	19	10	3	1	3	9	11	20
Brentford	15	4	3	0	16	5	2	4	2	11	12	19
Workington	15	2	5	1	9	6	3	3	1	3	1	18
Halifax Town	15	5	0	2	14	8	3	2	3	8	8	18
Lincoln City	16	5	1	2	16	7	2	3	3	5	13	18
Bradford City	15	5	1	1	16	5	1	4	3	8	15	17
Swansea Town	15	2	4	1	8	7	4	1	3	9	9	17
ROCHDALE	**15**	**2**	**4**	**1**	**11**	**5**	**1**	**6**	**1**	**6**	**6**	**16**
Wrexham	15	5	1	1	13	4	1	3	4	5	8	16
Colchester United	15	3	2	2	5	7	3	2	3	11	14	16
Southend United	15	5	1	1	15	6	0	4	4	8	14	15
Newport County	15	4	3	1	13	7	1	1	5	7	11	14
Peterborough United	15	4	3	1	14	9	0	2	5	3	9	13
Exeter City	16	2	5	1	13	9	1	2	5	8	17	13
Port Vale	15	4	3	1	12	6	0	1	6	3	13	12
York City	15	3	4	0	11	7	0	2	6	3	21	12
Scunthorpe United	15	3	2	2	9	8	1	1	6	16	20	11
Chesterfield	16	2	2	4	7	9	2	1	5	6	14	11
Grimsby Town	15	2	2	4	7	7	0	3	4	3	11	9
Notts County	15	1	2	4	6	12	1	2	5	8	17	8
Bradford Park Avenue	16	1	5	3	8	13	0	0	7	5	23	7

6.

NOVEMBER 1968

*Yesterday, all my troubles seemed so far away,
Now it looks as though they're here to stay.
Oh I believe in Yesterday.*
Paul McCartney (1965)

The month began auspiciously for world peace as President Johnson, "LBJ", ordered a total and unconditional end to the bombing of North Vietnam in an attempt to breathe life into the stalled peace talks in Paris. In return, the North Vietnamese agreed to allow the South Vietnamese to take part in the Paris talks but some cynics saw it as merely a ploy to help Vice-President Humphreys' chances in the forthcoming Presidential elections. From a personal viewpoint, there was anything but a cessation in bombing as a building site on nearby Cook Street was targeted by my cronies and I and subjected to daily assault by fireworks. Within minutes of the workmen leaving the site each day, we would climb the scaffolding to drop bangers down the hollow poles and await the amplified explosion. One evening, disgracefully and probably criminally, we totally wrecked a newly-laid concrete foundation by lobbing lit bangers into the wet substance from the top of the scaffolding and creating a passable impression of a lunar landscape as a consequence. In retrospect, it is a wonder that we were never apprehended. Maybe the matter was not reported to the Police (good job too for yours truly!) but a worse fate surely would have been to be caught by the workmen whose labours had been so cruelly vandalised. As I (the picture of innocence) walked by the site one morning on my way to call for John, my bowels turned to water as I overheard a huge Irishman say "If Oi get moi hands on

NOVEMBER 1968

the little bas***ds what did this, Oi'll fec***g kill 'em!'". Our own ceasefire came into effect that day! Purely coincidentally, the Number 1 in the charts that week was Joe Cocker's version of the song from the Beatles' Sergeant Pepper album "With a Little Help from my Friends". Oops!

Almost equally explosive was Rochdale's performance in their first match in November as they creamed the other Bradford club, Park Avenue, by six goals to nil and, of course, I was **not there** to witness it! This time I was thwarted by the wedding of some obscure relative somewhere in the Tameside area and heard of the result as we arrived at the reception. The second occasion this season on which my team had scored six and I'd missed them both - conspiracy theories abounded! Again relatives suggested that, if I loved my team, I would stay away for the rest of the season, thereby guaranteeing the Dale promotion! My only consolation, scant as it was, came in taunting my Uncle Frank, a staunch Manchester City fan, after his side lost 0-2 at Chelsea.

Saturday 2nd November
ROCHDALE 6 BRADFORD P.A. 0
(Division 4)

Attendance: 2,795 Referee: Mr. W. Handley (Cannock, Staffs.) H-T: 3-0

Harker
Radcliffe   Parry   Smith   Ryder
Leech   Rudd
Whitehead   Melledew   Melling   Butler
(Jenkins was an unused substitute)

This was a comprehensive and one-sided victory over a desperately-poor Park Avenue side who, although we did not of course realise at this time, were in their penultimate season as a League team. **Melling** opened the scoring as early as the 8th minute

ECHOES OF '69

as he forced in Butler's cross from the by-line, his first for the club. Then, in the 15th minute and again from Butler's pull-back, **Rudd** chipped over the 'keeper. **Melledew** scored his, by now, customary goal after 30 minutes but it took Rochdale a further 40 minutes before they were able to add to their tally. This time, a short corner routine between Butler and Whitehead provided **Radcliffe** with a chance which he hammered home (also **his** first goal for the club). After 83 minutes, the fifth goal came courtesy of **Butler's** penalty kick after Leech had been brought down in the area and the scoring was rounded off by a brilliant **Rudd** volley, his second, again following a Butler and Whitehead short corner routine. The Dale defence was never under any threat throughout the game. As the Observer reported; "Colin Parry and Graham Smith took part in the proceedings. *They, like Harker, have probably used up more energy in practice games!"*. What a match! What a result! What a chump for not being there AGAIN when the Dale scored six!

Inspired by this stirring victory, and because it was half-term, I succeeded in persuading my parents to let me attend the Dale's next game which was on the Monday evening (YES! Precedent firmly established; ten out of ten for perseverance!). As Newport were languishing around 15th position in the table, with a far from impressive away record showing only one win so far this season, I bowled my way up to Spotland fully expecting another scintillating six-goal performance, only this time, as Arthur Askey would have said "..before my very eyes!". How wrong I would be!

Monday 4th November
ROCHDALE 0 NEWPORT COUNTY 1
(Division 4)

Attendance: 4,223 Referee: Mr. W. Handley (Cannock, Staffs.) H-T: 0-0

Harker
Radcliffe   **Parry**   **Ashworth**   **Ryder**

NOVEMBER 1968

Smith   Rudd
Whitehead   Melledew   Melling   Butler
(Jenkins as substitute replaced Melling after 80 minutes)

Rochdale enjoyed territorial superiority throughout an error-strewn first half but goals again failed to materialise. In the second half Melledew was clearly pulled back by a Newport defender but did not go down and no penalty was awarded. Then, ten minutes from time, Hill scored for the visitors with an innocuous 20 yard drive. One thing that I do remember from the game was the way the Rochdale supporters "gave the bird" to the Newport centre-forward, Tony Buck (who we will meet later in this narrative). I think it was because he was blonde and useful - these days I prefer those qualities in my women!

Poignantly, the new Number 1 in this week's charts had a title which accurately summed up Dale's season so far (and predicted its nosedive between this point and Christmas). The title? "The Good, The Bad and The Ugly" by Hugo Montenegro's Orchestra - how utterly and compellingly appropriate!

An interesting development at this game saw the appearance on the ground of a rather dilapidated white caravan. Situated at the back of the ground, at the corner of the Wilbutts Lane "Scratching Shed" and the Pearl Street partially-covered terrace, this functioned as an in-ground Club Shop selling a small range of Rochdale merchandise, such as it was. However, far more importantly to the author, it also stocked old football programmes from a variety of clubs and, from this source, developed a passion which has stayed with me to the present day. Little did I know, back in 1968, when I was spending my pocket money buying the odd programme from Southampton or Newcastle United simply because they were exotic and distant (from Rochdale's viewpoint both geographically and philosophically) that, thirty-odd years on, I would possess a collection with a conservative valuation of £16,000 and growing. Today, when my wife Lynn jokingly says to me "Are you playing with your programmes again?",

ECHOES OF '69

I trot out my habitual retort about them being an investment and how much profit I've made on them "on paper". Of course, this really is total bollocks! I will never realise the investment or the notional profit by virtue of the simple fact that I will never sell my collection. It is an essential part of Steve Jones, the person. The Collection, as it happens, is specifically bequeathed in my Will to my son Greg. It is not merely a hobby or an investment mechanism; rather it is a compulsion. It is axiomatic that all men (or over-aged schoolboys if you prefer) have a psychological need to foster a compulsion; this is mine. My stance is that, as I don't go to the Pub every night, or chase women, or buy and re-sell old cars, I have found a personal outlet for that certain peculiar eccentricity that we all possess to differing degrees. The only downside is that I'm fast running out of storage space in my study; 8,000+ football programmes take up rather a lot of shelf space! All of this apparently kicked off by the appearance of a dilapidated white caravan - spooky!

A rather more important event, in the greater scheme of things, occurred a couple of days later when Richard Milhous Nixon, the Republican candidate, won the election to become America's next President. His running-mate, and therefore future Vice-President, was the curiously named (and, it would later transpire, equally "economical with the truth") Spiro T. Agnew.

Domestically, front page news in the Rochdale Observer this weekend was made by the sale of a house. Set in two acres of grounds, the property "Sevenoaks", on Meadowcroft Lane, Bamford, reached an unprecedented £20,000 at auction. For our entertainment and edification, showing at the Odeon cinema was that blockbuster (?) "Prudence and the Pill", starring David Niven and Deborah Kerr. This x-rated movie prided itself on "the first comedy about the contraceptive pill". I was not in the least bit offended by or interested in this. Some two years earlier, I had become an expert in "the facts of life", courtesy of classmate Howard Royds, who had shared with me all his vast knowledge of procreation in exchange for a packet of KP peanuts.

NOVEMBER 1968

Back to matters footballing, and the Dale were looking to put their latest disappointment behind them with a good performance at then second-placed Aldershot.

Saturday 9th November
ALDERSHOT 0 ROCHDALE 0
(Division 4)

Attendance: 5,183 Referee: Mr. R. Spittle (Great Yarmouth) H-T: 0-0

Harker
Radcliffe   Parry   Smith   Ryder
Leech   Rudd
Whitehead   Melledew   Jenkins   Butler
(Fletcher was an unused substitute)

Melling was dropped for the game having scored just once in eleven appearances and it proved another exercise in defensive strength as the Dale collected another hard-earned away point. Harker was, by some distance, the man of the match following a string of fine saves but, again, the absence of much action to report gave the Observer's correspondent (this time it was back to Geoff Whitworth) the opportunity to be hyperbolic (trust me, it is OK to use this word in mixed company!). This week's quotable prose went: *"In the last seconds, Billy Rudd twinkled (sic) into the Aldershot penalty area to be stopped by Renwick flipping him to the ground with a throw straight out of the Judo text book. The linesman, who had a ringside seat, unhesitatingly signalled for a foul but, just as swiftly, lowered his raised flag"*. In retrospect, the Aldershot team contained a few names that Dale fans would come to "know and boo". Trainer Dick Connor, would become Number 2 at Spotland less than a month later whilst the team itself contained future Dale legends (or should that be leg ends?) Tony Godfrey, Dick Renwick, Jack Howarth and Peter Gowans.

ECHOES OF '69

During the following week, John and I got a bee in our respective bonnets that it would be a pretty cool thing to do to go and watch the Dale play in an away game. We each told our own parents that the other's parents said it was "alright with them" and, miracle of miracles, it worked like a dream! The next day, my dad took us to the office of Ellen Smith's Coaches on Yorkshire Street, Heybrook to allow us to book our tickets for the next Saturday's excursion to Barnsley for a First Round F.A.Cup tie. Now, Ellen Smith's garage was already well known to me as my dad had bought his petrol there ever since we had owned a car and the manager, Harry Smith, was a real character. He was a remarkable man for two reasons. Firstly, his orthodontics were incredible. He possessed an array of teeth, no two of which were identical, and which was reminiscent of a broken piano keyboard (one black, one white, one missing!). Secondly, and much more important, he had the kind of childish sense of humour that enables some adults to communicate so brilliantly with young kids. At age eight or so, this guy had strung me along for maybe six or nine months solemnly telling me that *"..there is no Ellen Smith"* until I twigged that he was saying *"there is no "L" in SMITH"!* Thereafter, every time we bowled up at the garage without my mother he would have me in tucks of laughter by conspiratorially winking at me and saying *"Have you not got the Queen Bee with you today then?"*- it wasn't that it was particularly funny, it's more that, aged eight or nine, he made me feel like "one of the lads". Anyway, after obtaining my solemn promises not to slash any seats, or pee in the stairwell, or swear, or show my arse out of the coach window, he agreed to sell the tickets to John and I (to this day I remember the price; 7/6d full fare and 3/9d concessions). The intervening days at school dragged on interminably as we couldn't wait for Saturday to come. Fellow Dale supporters at school could not believe that we were being allowed to go - "Eeh, we thowt it wur grand!".

Eventually, Saturday morning dawned and it was time to meet up at the Coach Station for the 12:30 departure. It was a typically frosty and foggy November day (there was even fear expressed that the match might be postponed when we got to Barnsley) and I have a recollection

NOVEMBER 1968

that it took about two hours to get there. Today, with the M60, M62 and M1 access it takes just 45 minutes (I know this because I made a rather nostalgic return journey just four months ago when I took Greg and three of his schoolmates to Oakwell to see England Under-19s play their Hungarian counterparts - God! How the place had changed!). Today's Oakwell is an all-seater stadium with three new stands and executive boxes. In 1968, it had a pokey little wooden stand and the rest was terracing apparently built by laying wooden railway sleepers on a slag heap thrown up from the local coal pits. Indeed I well recall some Barnsley fans outside the ground with coal-blackened faces who must obviously have come to the match straight from a shift "down t'pit". It must have been apparent that John and I were "away match virgins" as one "handy-looking" Dale fan advised us to move from our position behind the goals to a spot near the corner flag "just in case any unpleasantness started" with the Barnsley fans! In the event, nothing at all untoward occurred as we took in the delights of seeing our team more than hold their own against higher-league opposition, and also experienced being the minority support in a vocally hostile environment. (We would experience this many more times in years to come - sadly, often at Spotland as home support withered and "big" clubs brought along large travelling support; Aston Villa, Preston, Bolton and Blackburn springing readily to mind.)

Saturday 16th November
BARNSLEY 0 ROCHDALE 0
(FA CUP 1st Round)

Attendance: 11,414 Referee: Mr. J.Quinn (Middlesbrough) H-T: 0-0

Harker
Radcliffe   Parry   Ashworth   Ryder
Leech   Rudd
Whitehead   Melledew   Smith   Butler

(Jenkins as substitute replaced Smith after 74 minutes)

ECHOES OF '69

The team line-up caused a bit of a stir when it was announced, most people wrongly assuming that Smith would adopt a defensive role when, in fact, he did a commendable job up front. Despite this, however, Rochdale were again unable to convert any of the chances that came their way but, as we piled back onto our coach for the journey home, we took comfort in the fact that we would be in the draw for the Second Round of the Cup for the first time since 1965 (then we had just drawn 2-2 with Fleetwood of the Football Combination!). Of course, in those days, FA Cup draws were held on Monday lunchtime following the weekend games and broadcast only on the radio, unlike today when it sometimes seems that half of the games from the current round have still to be played and the draw is merely another opportunity for David Davies of the F.A to get his smug phizog on the box! The journey home was notable only for the outbreak on the back seat of a spontaneous display of synchronised farting as some older supporters combated the dual effects of "Barnsley Bitter" and "Hirst's celebrated pork pies", both of which were heavily featured in the match programme! Incongruously, the same page featured an advertisement for Chanel perfume (courtesy of Arthur Wright & Son, Dispensing Chemists) and by the end of the journey, the atmosphere on the coach would certainly have benefited from a liberal application of Eau de Cologne to replace the all-pervading "Odour over-indulgence"! Despite this, John and I thought it a brilliant day out and vowed to repeat it as soon as we could afford it.

The journey home seemed a lot shorter and meant that there were still a variety of televisual feasts to be enjoyed for the rest of the weekend, not least of which were the following (how many of these do you recall without a lump appearing in the throat, either nostalgia or nausea?):

"Dixon of Dock Green" (dear old Jack Warner was still to be pensioned off)

"Dee Time" (the eponymous Simon Dee, a cult figure of his time. No Madam, "cult"!)

NOVEMBER 1968

"The Val Doonican Show" (remember the pullovers and cardigans?)

"The Forsyte Saga" (Part Eleven was screened this particular weekend; I'm not sure if this was the one where Soames did something unspeakable to Fleur!)

"'Til Death Us Do Part" (the "Scarse git" is now "President" Blair's father-in-law)

"Rowan and Martin's Laugh-in" ("..very interesting, but stupid"!)

"Joe 90" (who, I have to confess, could have been modelled on me aged twelve!).

And so onto the replay with hopes high for a small act of "giant-killing".

Monday 18th November
ROCHDALE 0 BARNSLEY 1
(FA CUP Replay)

Attendance: 7,340 Referee: Mr. J. Quinn (Middlesbrough) H-T: 0-1

Harker
Radcliffe   Parry   Ashworth   Ryder
Leech   Rudd
Whitehead   Melledew   Smith   Butler

(Jenkins as substitute replaced Smith after 74 minutes)

In the end it wasn't to be, as the Dale were mugged on the night! A breakaway goal by Dean in the first half for Barnsley (described as an "ambush" by the Ob) allied to Rochdale's chronic inability to score (this was their fourth consecutive game without a goal) conspired to deprive us of a second round cup appearance for yet another year. At least I managed to get to the game, the principle and precedent of attending weekday matches now being firmly established, but this one had not been a match to treasure.

ECHOES OF '69

So it was back to the bread and butter of the league campaign. The club hierarchy was obviously concerned at the poor goal scoring record and an apparently sizeable bid had been tabled to attempt to bring Alex Dawson from neighbours Bury. Dawson, a former Busby Babe, had been prematurely promoted from the Youth team into the immediately post-Munich United team and, indeed, played on the right wing in the 1958 Cup Final versus Bolton Wanderers. The protracted negotiations took up a lot of column space in the local paper but, eventually, any deal was called off as the clubs failed to reach an agreement. Clearly Len Richley would have to "make do" with the existing personnel at the club.

Saturday 23rd November
WREXHAM 3 ROCHDALE 2
(Division 4)

Attendance: 3,412   Referee: Mr. R. Jennings (Stockbridge)   H-T: 2-1

Harker
Radcliffe   Parry   Ashworth   Ryder
Leech   Rudd
Whitehead   Melledew   Melling   Butler

(Smith was an unused substitute)

Melling was offered a further chance to prove himself but, unusually, it was the defence that gave most cause for concern in this match. Griffiths put the home side ahead after 23 minutes and, within a minute, May had scored a second with a header. It could have been worse; Radcliffe kicked a shot off the line before **Melling** headed in Whitehead's centre just before half-time. Rochdale's fight back continued and, on the hour, **Melling** again got on the end of Whitehead's cross for the equaliser. It was to prove all in vain, however, as Radcliffe was again "skinned" by

NOVEMBER 1968

Griffiths who planted his cross on Kinsey's head for the winner with five minutes remaining. It had been a stirring effort by the Dale but, in conceding three goals in a game for the first time in the season, they had set themselves too high a target to get anything out of the game.

Monday evening saw the second replay in the saga that was the Lancashire Cup 1st round. This time the Latics squeezed out a 1-0 victory over a Dale side featuring Fletcher in place of Melledew as the only change from that beaten by Wrexham.

Back at school, "Double Art" on Tuesday morning proved to be the highlight of the week as our bearded wonder, leather elbow-patched, arty-farty type teacher Mr. Clarke (does my mind play tricks or did he really wear a psychedelic-patterned cravat?), was prevailed upon to let us play the brand new Beatles album (the White Album) throughout the lesson. I can't be sure precisely what I was doing at this time, but I have a vague recollection of sitting at the potter's wheel and turning (no pun intended!) a once-promising vase or urn into a rather disappointing imploded ashtray. Sadly, Art was never my best subject, otherwise I could have combined it with my Maths and eventually got a job painting computers! The "Beatles Appreciation" classes would continue right through to Christmas and, to this day, I would still rank the White Album as my favourite of all the Beatles' albums. It doesn't contain any of the major singles hits ("Back in the USSR" and a version of "Revolution" being the only songs issued in this medium) but for the sheer variety of music styles contained within it, this is a showcase for the individual Beatles' musical talents. Where else could you find an album containing such diverse elements as "Blackbird" and "Helter Skelter", or " While My Guitar Gently Weeps" and "Birthday"? Looking back, I see now how these Art lessons were a major influencing factor in developing my discerning and catholic taste in music. Thank you, bearded one!

ECHOES OF '69

Saturday 30th November
ROCHDALE 0 NOTTS COUNTY 0
(Division 4)

Attendance: 2,673   Referee: Mr. Williams (Sheffield)   H-T: 0-0

Harker
Radcliffe   Parry   Smith   Ryder
Ashworth   Rudd
Whitehead Fletcher Melling Butler

(Melledew as substitute replaced Butler after 80 minutes)

I have only a dim recollection of this game which has little to do with the football. Rather it is a memory of a feeling of hopelessness that a season, which had promised so much initially, was now fast going down the pan. A memory of a feeling of depression settling over the ground during the match where the team, missing the influential Leech in midfield and replacing him with the wholehearted but limited Ashworth, was unable to conjure up anything remotely entertaining for the lowest crowd of the season. The Rochdale Observer summed it up in describing the team as "…carrying its confidence in a colander". Smith hit the bar in the last five minutes of the game but that summed up the action. We didn't know it at the time, but this would be the last time we would see the Dale in 1968 and, as John and I made our way home, cold damp and miserable after the game, we would surely have questioned whether or not there was a better way to spend a winter's afternoon than trekking up to Spotland.

NOVEMBER 1968

The result left Rochdale in thirteenth position in the Division, with the full table looking like this:

FOOTBALL LEAGUE DIVISION 4
November 30, 1968

	P	W	D	L	F	A	PTS
Darlington	20	9	9	2	28	13	27
Aldershot	20	11	4	5	33	24	26
Doncaster Rovers	20	11	3	6	32	27	26
Lincoln City	21	10	5	6	26	23	25
Workington	20	8	8	4	19	13	24
Swansea Town	20	8	7	5	21	19	23
Chester	20	8	6	6	35	27	22
Southend United	20	8	6	6	30	26	22
Brentford	20	7	8	5	32	24	22
Colchester United	20	9	4	7	26	26	22
Halifax Town	19	9	4	6	26	21	22
Bradford City	19	7	7	5	27	24	21
ROCHDALE	**20**	**4**	**12**	**4**	**25**	**15**	**20**
Peterborough United	20	6	7	7	28	24	19
Newport County	20	6	7	7	24	22	19
Wrexham	19	7	5	8	23	19	19
Port Vale	20	6	7	7	21	22	19
Exeter City	22	5	8	9	29	34	18
Scunthorpe United	20	7	4	9	31	31	18
Chesterfield	21	6	5	10	20	28	17
York City	20	4	8	8	17	35	16
Grimsby Town	20	4	7	9	19	24	15
Notts County	19	3	5	11	17	32	11
Bradford Park Avenue	21	2	5	14	16	52	9

7.

DECEMBER 1968

*T'was the night before Christmas and all through the house,
Not a creature was stirring, just a burglar, a scouse.*
Man. United fan, 1988.

In any school the run-up to Christmas is a busy and hectic time fraught with tension. This description aptly fitted Howarth Cross in December 1968, not least for those members of class 3A1 who were involved in no less than two "theatrical" productions for the entertainment and edification of the rest of the school. In the first of these, the French teacher (the lovely Miss Clarke, who subsequently would recklessly unleash me and my contemporaries on the unsuspecting burghers of Paris and Biarritz on a school holiday the following June), had the brilliant idea of performing a version of Cinderella in French. Yours truly ended up being cast as "Buttons", which I took to be a reflection of my developing linguistic skills (in later years, I would be labelled a cunning linguist because I could get my tongue around anything!). If not that, then the casting was due to the comic potential envisaged in linking me up with the leading lady (the eponymous "Cendrillon") who towered over me by a good nine inches, and under whose enormous breasts I could easily have sheltered, completely dry, if there had been a sudden cloudburst! I should explain at this juncture that I was not particularly small for my age but the rest of my classmates tended, for the most part, to be a year older than me. I had had the (mis)fortune to be promoted by one academic year during what transpired to be my last year at Junior school - a decision made as

DECEMBER 1968

much for reasons of balancing class sizes as perceived intellectual ability or potential, I'm sure. As "Buttons", I played a sort of narrator role, which meant that I had more lines than the rest of the cast put together. Consequently, home-life was tense for a couple of weeks as I spent most of my spare time learning and rehearsing the part, which was difficult as no bugger else in the household spoke French! Eventually, however, the performances themselves went well, with a separate show for each of Years 1, 2 and 3. A slightly unusual feature was that, having done the play in French, we would then repeat the whole thing in English (presumably for the benefit of the remedial classes, who were not taught French and who would otherwise have thought that their dyslexia had developed aural dimensions).

The second production was another attempt to show what clever little ba***rds class 3A1 were (!) by performing a version of Snow White and the Seven Dwarfs (or Woe Snite and the Devon Swarfs, for any dyslexic reader who might have been offended by my last comment!) in, wait for it, LATIN! Mr. Ashworth, the school's deputy headmaster, took us for Latin and obviously had far too much time on his hands when he undertook to provide a translated script for this spectacle. I was type-cast as a dwarf (it was probably Dopey, but this is a memory I had all but erased, on the grounds of taste, so I can't be certain) so at least I did not have too many lines to learn. We (that is, the dwarfs) did, however, have to perform a musical number (I'm cringeing now merely writing this!) - the "Hi-Ho" song as featured in the Disney film animation of the story. Incredibly, and inexplicably, I can still remember the opening lines of the refrain (is this sad or what?) : *"Hi Ho, Hi Ho. Domum iam ibo! Cum baculo, cum saculo, Hi Ho, Hi Ho, Hi Ho, Hi Ho"*. If memory serves correct, this literally translates as "I am going home, with a stick and with a bag" (!) but at least it scanned well with the tune. We gave but one performance, before the whole school, to deafening silence and I am left with a mental picture of two hundred kids sat squirming with suppressed glee, each with a little thought

ECHOES OF '69

balloon above their heads containing the words "what the f*** was all that about?". I will draw a line under this event now, and work hard on finally erasing the memory.

The theme tune to "The Good, The Bad and the Ugly" was still Number 1 in the charts for the first two weeks of December, and we Dale supporters were now very much at the truly ugly stage of our season. The team had been taken to the nearby resort of Skegness a couple of days ahead of the game at Grimsby to give them a break in routine and help to bind team spirit. The only absentee was Billy Rudd, who stayed behind to nurse his wife who was convalescing after having her tonsils removed (possibly by one of his tackles, it was suggested!).

Saturday 7th December
GRIMSBY TOWN 2 ROCHDALE 0
(Division 4)

Attendance: 2,517 Referee: Mr. J. Hunting (Leicester) H-T: 1-0

Harker
Radcliffe   Parry   Smith   Ryder
Ashworth   Melling   Rudd
Whitehead   Fletcher   Melledew

(Butler as substitute replaced Ashworth after 66 minutes)

Tactically, Dale were undone by Grimsby's six foot four and a half inch centre forward Walker, who had recently been plucked from the obscurity of amateur football. He scored with headers, naturally, in the 22nd and 81st minutes. In between times, Fletcher's penalty, on the stroke of half-time, was saved by the Grimsby keeper, and Melling, who had a very effective game in midfield, hit the bar in the first twenty minutes. These exceptions apart, however, Rochdale were rarely in the game and, far from talking about promotion potential, supporters were anxiously looking at the

DECEMBER 1968

number of points safety-net which existed above the re-election places.

On the Tuesday following the game, Dick Connor assumed his duties as trainer/coach at the club after the formalities of his move from Aldershot had been finalised. He would subsequently manage the team between 1970 and 1973. It was also reported that Bury had sold Alex Dawson to Brighton for £10,000, at the same time disclosing that Rochdale's abortive bid had been in the region of £6,000.

As Christmas drew inexorably closer and the daylight hours grew shorter, opportunities for playing out were severely restricted. Despite the pleasure of trying to work out the lyrics to the new Number One, "Lily the Pink" by The Scaffold, even twelve year old lads have a tolerance threshold for playing Subbuteo, which is generally between five and six hours before you start to get a little cheesed off. Fortunately, relief was found in a board game that my mate John retrieved one day from a long-forgotten corner of his toy cupboard. The game in question was called "Formula One" and, as the name suggests, was a Grand Prix motor racing simulation featuring a six-lane track on a board, around which you had to pilot your own plastic miniature racing car. The game was an exercise in logic and tactics, the more dastardly the better, and not in any way dependent upon chance, either by throwing dice or turning over chance cards. We whiled away many hours sat at the Dining Room table, incurring brake and tyre wear penalties, baulking each other and causing spin-offs and retirements - if anyone out there has still got a version of the game that they want to sell, give me a call! If you don't want to sell it, maybe I could just pop round for an hour....?

Rochdale's next game was scheduled to be a home match versus Darlington on Saturday 14th December but the night before brought a very hard ground frost. Local referee Jim Cattlin (who, coincidentally but unbeknownst to me at the time, was a good friend of my parents until his recent passing) had no alternative but to call

ECHOES OF '69

off the game and, consequently, prevent the Darlington team and their supporters travelling. By 5:00pm, the Dale had fallen to thirteenth position in the Division table.

The forthcoming end of term would also bring the 3rd Year Christmas party, a very adult affair running from 7:30 to 10:00pm. Just how seriously this event was taken can be gauged by the number of periods given over to "dancing practice", although P.E. or Games were the usual subjects sacrificed. The "dancing" in question mainly consisted of "the barn dance", but it was better than you might think because we, trendy swingers that we were in this increasingly permissive age, did it "progressive-style". Sadly, this is not to be interpreted as us dancing to Syd Barrett-inspired Pink Floyd or early Led Zeppelin; it simply means that, after each sequence of steps, the female shuffled off to the right and danced with the next lad in line. Clearly, the big advantage here was that you got to grab hold of all the "top totty" in 3rd year (or whatever the popular vernacular term was in 1968; "groovy chicks" or "gear birds" presumably!). Conversely, and on the downside, you also "copped for a tug" from time to time. Whilst this expression conjures up visions of mild sexual assault, I should explain that the word "tug" in this context is a pejorative and highly derogatory term usually applied to the best friend of an attractive girl. More explanation needed? Well, if you picture a sleek, gleaming ocean-going yacht or cruise-liner coming in to dock, what does it need as support, to get it in its proper position and, at the same time, make it look better than it really is? The answer is - a tug! English lessons with Mr. Tinkler had taught me that this is a metaphor. The lascivious side of my character needed no prompting that this was an opportunity to get to close quarters with the (non-identical) Earnshaw twins from 3A2 (especially the marginally prettier Lesley). Still two months short of my thirteenth birthday, I reached the life-changing realisation that girls were "different". Not simply because they couldn't kick a ball without falling over, whistle in tune or ride a bike with a crossbar, but they smelled nice (once you

Footballing author in 1920s cigarette card pose.

Birthday Boy: The author posing as Joe 90, with his sister Lindsay.

Two cheeky monkeys... and two furry creatures!

1968-9 pre-season team group (pre-Buck and Melling).

Enjoying pre-season training: Ryder, Smith & Ashworth prominent.

Defence! Smith, Parry & Ashworth defend the 'Dale net.

Joe Ashworth & Reg Jenkins attacking a corner
at the Sandy Lane End.

Mudbath! Football as it used to be
(note the cloth caps among the spectators).

Tony Buck heads clear over his own bar.

Autographed team line-up
(original now worth millions!).

Lifting the Lancs.Cup in 1972: Gowans (with sideburns), Blair, Butler, Ashworth and Smith celebrate.

DECEMBER 1968

got close enough), they had much more interesting "mucky bits" (once you got bold enough), and kissing them manifested a very rapid and satisfactory surge in pre-pubescent growth which had nothing to do with my height! The mould was set and I was forever committed to the heterosexual path of life. Years later, in a pub toilet, I would see a piece of graffiti which said: "My mother made me a Homosexual!" to which someone had added, "If I sent her the wool, would she make me one?"). The dance passed off without serious incident, despite the almost overwhelming temptation provided by zip-front miniskirts, the current "in-thing". We all "did Coke", but in 1968, Coca-Cola was "the Real Thing" and too many strawberry Hubble Bubbles made you puke anyway. Maybe we didn't believe in Father Christmas any longer but, looking back, we seemed incredibly naïve compared to today's 12/13 year olds. Like the man said, nostalgia isn't what it used to be!

During the week it was announced that Vinnie Leech had been appointed Captain in place of Billy Rudd. The Dale's last game before Christmas would take them to Swansea and it was not the Christmas present that we were looking for (neither, frankly, was the "Rolf Harris Stylophone" which was on sale at Bradley's music shop at the bargain price of just £8/18/6).

Saturday 21st December
SWANSEA TOWN 3 ROCHDALE 0
(Division 4)

Attendance: 5,703 Referee: Mr. W. Castle (Dudley) H-T: 1-0

Harker
Radcliffe   Parry   Ashworth   Ryder
Leech   Rudd
Whitehead   Jenkins   Melling   Butler
(Melledew was an unused substitute)

ECHOES OF '69

This was, in every sense, the lowest point of the season. The Dale fell behind after just seven minutes to a Williams header (albeit that there was the suspicion of a push on Ryder in the build-up). He then repeated the feat on 51 minutes, at the near post, and just minutes later, Briggs scored the third with yet another header. Geoff Whitworth, for the Rochdale Observer, was despondent; *"...one team buoyantly and adroitly riding the crest of a self-made wave, the other sliding deeper into a trough equally of their own making"*. We had now gone nine games without a win (including the Lancashire Cup games against Oldham) and scored only two goals in that time (and both of those in a match against Wrexham that had been lost). The slide had taken the Dale down as low as fifteenth position in the table and, worryingly, there were now a mere two points separating us from York City who were 22nd. What would Christmas bring by way of cheer?

For three American astronauts, there was a Christmas away from home with a difference. Apollo VIII was launched on 21st December from Cape Kennedy and its six day mission included ten orbits of the moon. This was fascinating stuff, literally history in the making, as the craft entered the Moon's gravity and the world collectively seemed to hold its breath during the period of natural radio silence as it disappeared behind the Moon (later we would see the first ever pictures of the inappropriately named "Dark Side").

The Christmas routine in the Jones household was pretty well established. Early morning on Christmas Day, my sister Lindsay and I would sit at the bottom of the stairs whilst Mum and Dad, on an advance scouting mission, checked the lounge to confirm that "Father Christmas had been" (old habits die hard - I now do exactly the same thing every year with my son Greg). Only then could we dash in and start to attack the copious pile of presents that awaited us. Parents certainly have idiosyncratic ways with their kids. In my later teens, one of my friends, who for obvious reasons will remain nameless, invited me round to his house. When I got there, I noticed that, on the mantelpiece, his mother had a framed photograph of

DECEMBER 1968

him tightly grasping his penis. She kept it there until he was turned seventeen. How embarrassing can you get? - it must have been there almost twelve months! But I digress. On Christmas Day, my maternal grandparents came to us for traditional dinner, after which we would watch TV and the Queen's speech. Televisual highlights this year included; *"The Black and White Minstrel Xmas Show"*; the annual *"Top of the Pops Review of the Year"*; *"Doddy for Xmas"* and *"Stingray"*. Wow! How fantastic (this is irony!), but these days were pre-Morecambe & Wise Christmas Show - a time when the English were still not entirely comfortable with enjoying themselves on Christmas Day. I have earlier recollections of Christmas Days being spent at Arthur and Annie Newman's house, who were old friends/neighbours of my grandparents, but they emigrated to Australia in the early Sixties (probably so they could enjoy themselves!). One unchanging constant, however, was the Boxing Day party at my Grandma's. There was always a great pile of presents under the tree which we were forbidden from even touching until we had finished our meal (and all the pots had been washed!). Gran would then dish them out individually (and ceremonially) and that was her job done. Then, and only then, could she relax and enjoy herself. It was the only time of year that we met up with the Emersons. The father, Paddy, would invariably, later in the evening, fall down the tight stairs in my grandparents' small terraced house as a direct consequence of over-imbibation (these days, we'd say he was pissed), whilst his wife Vera ritually sang "Scarlet Ribbons" which always moved the womenfolk to tears (perpetuating the Lancashire female myth that "you haven't had a good time unless you've had a good scrike"). I would probably have spent the evening playing an improvised game of balloon tennis with Paul, the youngest of the Emerson's four kids, whilst surreptitiously sneaking swigs out of cans of Pale Ale (the ones that you had to pierce in two places on the lid - there were no ring pulls in those days). I don't recall too much telly-watching that day but we did have "Grandstand" on for the football results. My research

ECHOES OF '69

uncovered the fact that Eddie Wareing and egg-chasing (sorry, Rugby League) featured heavily in the programme, although clearly every expense had been spared as the live game was, incredibly, Featherstone Rovers v Hunslet! Once this was over, however, I nervously sat on the edge of my seat waiting for the Rochdale result to come through on "the tele-printer". As was usual, all the minor Scottish results seemed to come through first (did East Fife 5 Forfar 4 ever really happen, or is it an urban myth?) before eventually came **D4 WORKINGTON 1 ...** (then a pause for what seemed like minutes before the rest of the result)   **...ROCHDALE 1.** I remember thinking that this was not too bad a result, given recent form, so imagine my surprise when the classified results summary came on and announced that the Dale had actually won 2-1! Now that's what I call "goodwill to all men" - and it had been a rare "White Christmas"!

Thursday 26th December
WORKINGTON 1 ROCHDALE 2
(Division 4)

Attendance: 2,921 Referee: Mr. V. Batty (Helsby) H-T: 1-1

Harker
Smith   Parry   Ashworth   Ryder
Leech   Rudd
Whitehead   Melling   Jenkins   Butler

(Melledew was an unused substitute)

The BBC's confusion over the score would prove to have been a function of Rochdale having scored a very late winner. In treacherous underfoot conditions and blinding sun, the Dale had begun with Smith coming into the team for Radcliffe, who had had a wretched game at Swansea. After 16 minutes, and totally against the run of play, the home team scored when Harker seemed to lose

DECEMBER 1968

a speculative shot from Ogilvie in the sun (a rare occurrence at any time in Workington, but especially in December!). Rochdale were quickly back on level terms, however, as a high ball from Smith was headed on by Melling to **Jenkins**, who headed over the keeper for his first goal of the season from open play (his previous two having both been penalties in the opening game of the season). Despite an overwhelming proportion of possession in the second half, the Dale had nothing to show for their endeavours until, in the 87th minute, Rudd chipped a ball over two defenders to Butler who hit a through ball to Jenkins. Taking the ball in his stride **Jenkins** scored with a trademark rasping left foot drive. This was Workington's first home defeat since the opening day of the season and lifted the Dale to fourteenth place in the table. As usual, the Rochdale Observer could be relied upon for hyperbole, this time though it came in the form of the headline caption to the match report;

SANTA JENKINS AND ROCHDALE REINDEER DELIVER THEIR OWN PRESENT

On Saturday 28th December, the Dale had been due to stage a home game against Southend United but the North West was still bound in an icy grip with snow and sub-zero temperatures. Our old friend, local referee Jim Cattlin, was again drafted in (no pun intended) and had little alternative but to call the game off as the ground was "like concrete". So Rochdale had gone through the whole of December without a home game. For me the year finished with me confined to bed with the 'flu (my other Grandma, my Dad's mum, baby-sat my sister and I on New Year's Eve as my parents went out "on the razz") and the Dale ended the year in an inglorious fifteenth position, nine points behind leaders Aldershot and five points away from a promotion place. The detailed table looked like this:

ECHOES OF '69

FOOTBALL LEAGUE DIVISION 4
December 31, 1968

	P	W	D	L	HOME F	A	W	D	AWAY L	F	A	Pts
Aldershot	23	7	2	3	20	11	6	3	2	20	14	31
Darlington	21	5	4	2	16	8	4	6	0	12	5	28
Lincoln City	24	8	1	3	21	8	3	5	4	8	17	28
Workington	23	4	6	2	15	9	5	3	3	7	7	27
Doncaster Rovers	23	7	3	2	21	13	4	2	5	12	15	27
Chester	23	8	2	2	27	11	2	4	5	17	21	26
Halifax Town	21	8	1	2	21	11	3	3	4	9	11	26
Southend United	23	8	1	2	22	9	2	5	5	13	21	26
Colchester United	22	7	2	2	16	9	4	2	5	16	20	26
Brentford	23	5	4	2	21	12	3	5	4	14	16	25
Swansea Town	24	4	5	2	13	12	5	2	6	12	15	25
Bradford City	23	6	4	2	20	9	1	5	5	9	20	23
Port Vale	24	7	4	2	18	10	1	3	7	6	16	23
Wrexham	22	7	1	2	18	7	1	5	6	7	12	22
ROCHDALE	**23**	**3**	**5**	**2**	**17**	**6**	**2**	**7**	**4**	**10**	**15**	**22**
Newport County	23	4	5	2	15	10	2	4	6	11	15	21
Peterborough United	22	6	4	1	22	11	0	4	7	9	17	20
Scunthorpe United	22	5	3	3	14	11	3	1	7	18	22	20
Chesterfield	25	3	5	5	13	14	3	3	6	10	18	20
York City	23	4	7	1	15	12	1	3	7	5	25	20
Grimsby Town	24	4	4	5	17	14	1	5	5	8	16	19
Notts County	23	4	3	4	14	16	2	4	6	11	19	19
Exeter City	25	3	6	3	19	14	2	2	9	12	27	18
Bradford Park Avenue	25	3	5	4	12	17	0	1	12	8	42	12

"**Should auld acquaintance be forgot and never brought to mind**" - it is remarkable that seven of the above teams are no longer League members (indeed some do not even exist in the same status), namely Aldershot, Workington, Chester, Halifax, Exeter, Newport and Bradford PA, whilst four others (Darlington, Lincoln, Doncaster and Colchester) have had a spell in non-League circles.

8.

JANUARY 1969

Football? It's the beautiful game!
Edson Arantes de Nascimento (Pele)

"O me miserum!" as my Latin teacher, Mr Ashworth, would have said; "woe is me". What a crappy start to the New Year! To get a dose of the 'flu is bad enough at any time but to get it during school holidays ... well! Even the jaunty melody of the first Number One pop song of the New Year, a version of the Beatles' "Ob-la-di, Ob-la-da" by Marmalade, was not enough to raise my spirits. I just wasn't up to it and I was going to miss another Saturday home game. Never mind, I thought, lightning cannot strike THREE times in the same place; surely the buggers couldn't score six again ... could they? Well, the message must have reached the players, "Right lads, Jonesy's not here- let's paste 'em!" because, incredibly, as I tuned in once more to Grandstand, the buggers DID score six again!! Was it me? Surely it had to be!

Saturday 4th January
ROCHDALE 6 GRIMSBY TOWN 1
(Division 4)

Attendance: 2,838 Referee: Mr. J. Hill (Macclesfield) H-T: 2-1

Harker
Smith   Parry   Ashworth   Ryder
Leech   Rudd
Whitehead   Melling   Jenkins   Butler
(Melledew was an unused substitute)

87

ECHOES OF '69

The scoring sequence (apparently!) went thus:

24 mins; **Melling** hooks home a corner kick, 1-0.
26 mins; A penalty is awarded against Parry for handball, and is duly converted, 1-1.
43 mins; Rudd is chopped down in the penalty area and **Jenkins** crashes home the resultant spot kick, 2-1.
51 mins; Whitehead's corner drops invitingly for **Jenkins** to score, 3-1.
62 mins; From Rudd's free-kick, the ball is lobbed into the net at the second attempt by **Whitehead** for his first competitive goal for the Dale, 4-1.
66 mins; Butler's cross is forced home by **Jenkins**, 5-1.
79 mins; A loose ball falls to **Rudd** who chips the 'keeper to score, **6-1. Six-bloody-one!**

So let's try and put this in perspective. The Dale's season found itself firmly back on track with this victory and this was the third time in the season that they had scored six goals in a home match - **and I had missed each and every one of them!** In fact, and I have checked this fact on a definitive spreadsheet listing that I keep of all the matches I attend, in the thirty-three years since, during which I have seen the Dale play nearly two hundred more times, I have **never** seen them score more than five in a game! I've seen United score nine and a couple of sevens at Old Trafford, I've seen Blackburn and Huddersfield each score seven at home. I went to Anfield just the once and Liverpool scored seven; that was depressing! I've even seen the Dale concede six at home (to Plymouth in 1973; fortunately I missed the 1-7 debacle versus Shrewsbury a couple of seasons back) but I have not seen them notch more than five. Is this a curse that I will carry to my grave, I ask myself?

Back at school on the Monday, following the Christmas break, all the talk centred around the improvement in the Dale's form and

JANUARY 1969

whether or not they could sustain it and mount a serious promotion push. John and I decided that, as the next game was away to Bradford PA - the bottom team in the League and against whom we had already scored six at home - we should make the short journey to see our team play. Accordingly, one evening after school, we again pitched up at Ellen Smith's garage at Wardleworth to book our tickets for the following Saturday - 5/6d for adults, 2/9d concessions, leaving at 1:30pm. There were two interesting sidelines during the rest of this week, both reported in the Rochdale Observer. In the first, David Cross had signed for the Dale as a part-time professional. Within a couple of years he would break into the first team before providing a financial lifeline for the club, when his sale to Norwich City realised £40,000 with Malcolm Darling as a makeweight in the deal. The second report was apropos of nothing in particular, but simply appealed to my warped sense of humour when I read it; *"The wheels, seats, carburettor, distributor and wheel discs were stolen during the weekend from a Triumph Spitfire sports car parked in Barrack Yard, Rochdale."*. What made me laugh was the headline caption which read simply:

"Spitfire Grounded!"

Saturday 11th January
BRADFORD P. A. 1 ROCHDALE 4
(Division 4)

Attendance: 5,453 Referee: Mr. R. Capey (Crewe) H-T: 1-1

Harker
Smith   Parry   Ashworth   Ryder
Leech   Rudd
Whitehead   Melling   Jenkins   Butler
(Riley was an unused substitute)

89

ECHOES OF '69

It was a bright but bitterly cold day as we travelled the short journey to Bradford and entered the ornate, but down-at-heel, Park Avenue ground. We found ourselves standing on terracing in front of a stand more reminiscent of a Victorian cricket pavilion which, in retrospect, it probably was given the dual nature history of the ground as both a football and cricket field (rather as Bramall Lane, Sheffield used to be). Standing up at a football match is a rarity these days, but it was only recently that I realised just how rare. Greg and I went to Halifax to watch the Dale in their ultimately-abortive promotion push (fingers crossed for the coming season as I type, which is tricky) and I asked him if he wanted to go in the seats or stand with the bulk of the Dale's travelling support. Now although only eleven years old, Greg has seen a lot of football (330 games to be precise) and his response absolutely staggered me. "Let's stand up Dad. I've never stood up at a football match" and it was a fact; every previous game he had seen had been from the comfort of the stands. How times change! Anyway back to Park Avenue, and one of the Bradford fans took an instant dislike to Terry Melling. He abused him mercilessly throughout the game with a string of curses, the least offensive (!) of which was to call him a "Mongolian Snot-gobbler". The match was recorded for ITV highlights the following day and I was convinced that I had heard this bloke's strident tones broadcast during the short excerpts of the game. It must have been this same guy who contributed to winding up Melling so much that I became the victim of his (retaliatory) abuse later in the game, as I described graphically in my introduction to this book. Needless to say, the expression "Chuck us that f***ing ball quick you tw*t!", became a stock phrase in our football kickabouts for the next few months (but always cunningly concealed from parents or other adults who might have been within earshot).

The game itself was a very entertaining affair, the more so if you were a Rochdale fan. After a slow start, the match sprang to life when a backpass from Whitehead was intercepted by Andrews

JANUARY 1969

who scored easily. This setback brought the desired response from the Dale and, in the 44th minute, **Whitehead** headed home after a misdirected punch by the Bradford 'keeper (Norman's goals, it would seem, were like buses or policemen - you saw none for ages then suddenly two would appear together!). Into the second half and it was Melling's turn for the spotlight as a Dale player scored a hat-trick for the second consecutive match (buses and policemen time again). In the 47th minute, Whitehead hung a cross up to the far post and there was **Melling** to head home. Then, with 61 minutes gone, Jenkins and Rudd combined on the left and the final ball into the box was forced in by **Melling** from close range. The hat-trick was completed when, again from a Whitehead cross, **Melling** was in the right place to tuck the ball home. The result (which was the Dale's best away win since 1956, or to put it another way, the best in my lifetime) took Rochdale up to tenth place in the table and we were starting to become a little giddy after three successive wins. Thoughts again began to turn to the possibility of a promotion push.

Away from football, the space programme (maybe that should be program, as it was American!) was hot news and the subject of much discussion and excitement at school. NASA announced that it had chosen Neil Armstrong and Edwin "Buzz" Aldrin for the first landing on the Moon to be undertaken later in the year. In the UK, sailings of the new cruise-liner Queen Elizabeth II, or QE2 as it became known, were cancelled because of trouble with her turbines and Ford Motors unveiled a new sports saloon, the Capri. This car would ultimately become a lifestyle icon, spawning jokes such as; *"How does an Essex girl turn off the light before having sex? By closing the door of her boyfriend's Capri!"*. On a more serious note, the world was appalled this month when, during continuing protests about the Russian occupation, a Czech student, Jan Palach, died in hospital two days after setting fire to himself in Wenceslas Square, Prague. Before he died he said, *"My act has fulfilled its purpose, but let nobody else do it"*. Poignant words indeed.

ECHOES OF '69

During this time at Howarth Cross, our Physics teacher Mr. Wall (or "Brick", as he was known - no madam, brick I said!) had the bright idea of setting up an Electronics Club one day per week after school. Take-up was low but I remember Barry Lord, Derek Harvey, and Terry Crabtree turning up most weeks. We played around with capacitors and resistors and melted lots of solder with our soldering iron, eventually producing working circuits that turned light bulbs on and off. I recall that we built an oscilloscope from a kit of some description which produced wavy green lines on a screen and noises like the soundtrack to Joe 90. My most vivid memory, however, was the occasion when we were allowed to mess around with a Van Der Graaf Generator which, without trying to be in any way technical, emits an electrical charge between two metal orbs. Obviously tiring rapidly of this piece of kit spitting a blueish flash (but doing little else, not even zapping any flies which might have strayed into its path) Barry Lord decided to put his head between the two orbs (ooh matron!). The result was spectacular as the electrical charge arced through the metal frames of his spectacles before earthing through the rubber soles of his shoes which he was luckily wearing! Fortunately there was no permanent damage, save for a few flashing lights in his vision over the next few hours and an interesting spikiness to his otherwise routine haircut. Was this an act of madness or genius in experimentation? I couldn't really say, all I know is that the same guy would eventually go to Cambridge where, after graduating, I believe he spent a number of years in research into Nuclear Fission! I just hope his experiments were a little more controlled by then.

Around the same time Miss Clarke, the French mistress (…Sorry, I had to have a short pause after typing those words, as the memory caused me to start to sweat and my hands to shake!) and Mr. Dixon, our other French teacher, announced that they would be taking a group of kids on holiday to France in June. The itinerary would see us spending two nights in Paris, seven nights in Biarritz and a further night in Paris on the way back. The parental "thumbs-

JANUARY 1969

up" having been obtained, and the £30 all-in cost duly paid, John and I discovered that the same Barry Lord would also be accompanying us on the trip.

Saturday 18th January
ROCHDALE 3 ALDERSHOT 0
(Division 4)

Attendance: 3,305   Referee: Mr. H. Davey (Mansfield)   H-T: 2-0

Harker
Smith   Parry   Ashworth   Ryder
Leech   Rudd
Whitehead   Melling   Melledew   Butler

(Riley was an unused substitute)

Aldershot arrived as leaders of the Division and the Dale were without "Big Reg" Jenkins (for what would otherwise have been his 300th League appearance), as he had been granted compassionate leave to attend his mother's funeral. It was another cold, damp and dismal day, which presumably contributed to the disappointing attendance, but our spirits were lifted by a brilliant performance from the boys in blue who completely outplayed their high-flying opponents. After 30 minutes, a Butler free-kick was dropped by Godfrey and **Melling** nodded the loose ball into the net (the expression "dropped by Godfrey" would, of course, feature in a few Rochdale match reports in future seasons). Six minutes later and Rudd's mazy run and cross saw Godfrey able only to palm the ball away (I rest my case!) and **Butler** followed up to tap in. The match was effectively over as a contest when, in the 57th minute, Rudd was scythed down in the area and **Butler** slammed home the resultant penalty. This, however, was one of those games where the goalscorers were overshadowed by the performance in midfield of Vinny Leech. Clearly revelling in his role as Captain, I recall him

ECHOES OF '69

seemingly covering every blade of mud (!) on the pitch and throwing himself into tackles which he had no right to win, yet emerging with the ball. This tenacity and will-to-win would be an inspiration to the team for the rest of the season.

I remember this game as the first time I had witnessed the always-amusing incident of the Tannoy-announcer asking for one of the turnstile-operators to "report to the Main Office immediately". The crowd's immediate reaction is always one of loud jeers of derision, with the implicit assumption that the said turnstile-operator has "legged it" with the takings, even if the actual need for his presence is quite legitimate. This got me thinking about the whole concept of Tannoy-announcers at football matches; today, in an era of conformity and increasingly anodyne blandness in football, the Tannoy-announcers stand out as a beacon of individuality and eccentricity. Ranging from the unutterably smug and polished (like the guy who does the England matches), through the stumblingly incompetent (the dyslexic guy Keegan?) at Old Trafford who audibly wets himself when he has to pronounce foreign names, and on to the down-right loopy guys who patently do the job because nobody else will! I've heard announcements that "the pies have come!", that "knickers in club colours with the official crest are available from the shop!" and, almost the best, the harassed guy who blurted out "How do you switch this f*****g thing on?", when clearly the microphone already was. As a boy of ten at Old Trafford I remember no less than three separate requests, in one game, for named spectators to "go home immediately as your wife has gone into labour" - personally I would have stayed to the final whistle, you're unlikely to miss anything in the first ninety minutes! However, the absolute best I ever heard was (also at Old Trafford some years ago) when the announcement came (to loud cheers) - "Will the owner of a blue Skoda, registration number XXXXX, parked in Car Park D, please return to his vehicle immediately ..... as it's on fire!". This was closely followed by another announcement (to even louder cheers and laughter) - "Will

JANUARY 1969

the owner of a silver Mercedes, registration number XXXXX, parked in Car Park D, please return to his vehicle immediately …. (long pause) AS IT'S PARKED NEXT TO THE SKODA!" Priceless!

There were two notable changes in leadership during this period. In America, Richard Nixon was sworn-in as President (this was nothing special - during this period I was often sworn-in at home when I omitted to wipe my muddy shoes!), whilst, six days earlier and far more importantly, Sir Matt Busby announced his retirement as Manchester United's manager, to be succeeded by Wilf McGuiness. In later years, I would have the privilege of being introduced to Wilf before a game at Old Trafford (I was the lucky recipient of some "Corporate Entertainment" at the time). As we were chatting, I asked him about some of his worst experiences in football and he launched into a story about how, after leaving United, he had gone coaching abroad in some Arab state, possibly Dubai, before returning to Bury as assistant manager. Things were not going well on the pitch and he went on to say; *"Behind the dug-out, I could hear people shouting 'F*** off back to the Middle East, McGuiness!', and that was just the wife and kids, the fans were worse!"*

The following Saturday (the 25th) should have seen the Dale travelling to play Newport County, but torrential rain had rendered the Somerton Park pitch unplayable and the game was postponed. It was already clear that fixture congestion would be a factor in the run-in to the end of the season but worse weather still was to come in February. For now we could relax and sit back listening to "Albatross" by Fleetwood Mac, which had finally replaced Marmalade at Number 1. In London, you would have had the unique opportunity to hear (if not see) the Beatles' last live performance when they cut a session for the film "Let it Be" on the rooftop of the Apple offices at 3, Savile Row. Before the plugs were pulled by the police who objected to the intrusive nature of loud rock music (coincidentally, this frequently happened to me at home!), Lennon had time to say that he "hoped they'd passed the audition".

ECHOES OF '69

As one of the worst winters on record dragged on, the Dale found themselves handily placed in eighth position, seven points behind the leaders and only four points off a promotion spot. Heady days, as the full table at the end of January shows.

FOOTBALL LEAGUE DIVISION 4
January 31, 1968

	P	W	D	L	F	A	W	D	L	F	A	PTS
		HOME					**AWAY**					
Aldershot	27	9	2	4	27	13	6	3	3	20	17	35
Doncaster Rovers	27	8	4	2	23	13	5	3	5	14	17	33
Lincoln City	28	9	2	3	25	11	3	7	4	10	19	33
Darlington	24	6	4	3	20	12	5	6	0	14	6	32
Colchester United	25	8	2	2	19	9	6	2	5	20	20	32
Chester	27	9	2	3	31	14	3	5	5	20	23	31
Workington	26	4	7	3	15	10	6	3	3	10	7	30
ROCHDALE	**26**	**5**	**5**	**2**	**26**	**7**	**3**	**7**	**4**	**14**	**16**	**28**
Halifax Town	24	8	1	3	21	15	3	5	4	10	12	28
Brentford	27	5	5	3	15	13	5	2	7	12	17	27
Bradford City	26	6	5	2	21	10	2	6	5	11	20	27
Swansea Town	27	5	5	3	15	13	5	2	7	12	17	27
Port Vale	26	8	4	2	23	10	1	4	7	6	16	26
Southend United	25	8	1	3	23	11	2	5	6	13	23	26
Wrexham	25	7	2	3	19	11	2	5	6	10	14	25
Scunthorpe United	25	6	3	3	16	12	4	1	8	19	24	24
Chesterfield	27	4	5	5	15	14	4	3	6	13	19	24
Newport County	26	5	5	2	19	12	2	4	8	11	24	23
York City	26	4	7	2	17	17	2	3	8	9	27	22
Peterborough United	26	6	5	2	24	14	0	4	9	12	23	21
Grimsby Town	28	4	4	7	18	17	2	5	6	14	24	21
Notts County	27	5	3	5	16	19	2	4	8	13	24	21
Exeter City	27	3	6	3	19	14	3	2	10	16	31	20
Bradford Park Avenue	28	3	6	5	13	21	0	1	13	8	45	13

9.

FEBRUARY 1969

Bar mitzvah - noun; a Jewish boy's bar mitzvah is a ceremony that takes place on his thirteenth birthday, after which he is regarded as an adult.
Collins New School Dictionary

As I approached **my** thirteenth birthday, I was in no immediate danger of being regarded as an adult (some might say that this is still the case thirty-odd years later). Puberty had rudely announced itself with an intermittently-breaking voice, a couple of blackheads erupting into volcanic facial protuberances and small wisps of hair in strategic locations, but I was still physically small. My sense of humour was essentially scatological (pooh/bum/titty allusions abounded) and my knowledge of the Jewish religion was confined to nudge-nudge references to circumcision (vis. Little Jewish Boy seen crying on the steps of the synagogue is approached by a policeman who asks "what is wrong?" LJB replies "Someone's nicked my pullover!". Fnarh! Fnarh!). However, I was starting to develop an increased awareness of my appearance and, more importantly, how this might be perceived by members of the opposite sex. This manifested itself in the wearing of "Sea Dogs" bell-bottom jeans and "Grandad Vest" T-shirts of various hues, although my favourite garment was a purple round-neck T-shirt commemorating the polar bear of the Cresta fizzy drinks brand uttering his catch-phrase "It's frothy, man!". There were also other, subtle signs of my developing maturity such as my rejection as "hideous" of a shirt my mother had bought for me. The fact that it was a dirty rust colour with cream cuffs and collar was reason enough (I'm sure you'd agree?), but it was the fact that I had had no input to the purchase decision itself which rankled with me most.

However, the single biggest inter-generational disharmony issue at this time was (and it would be for many years to come) that pertaining to my hair. At this point, it was not merely about the length or styling as I'd already progressed to going on my own to the "Razor's Edge" on Toad Lane where they trained wispy bits above your ears into "sideburns" (which would invariably stick out of your head at right angles when you woke up in a morning). This was light years away from Howarth's at the top of Hare Hill Road, Littleborough where my Dad had taken me "since Adam was a lad". There, despite the usual profusion of black and white blown-up pictures of male heads disporting varied hairstyles, everybody who went in eventually came out with the same haircut. "I'll have a Georgie Best, please". Snip, snip, snip. Electric razor on the back of the neck. Brush around the collar. The double-handled mirror held behind the head for inspection. Horrified shriek of "That's not a Georgie Best" would be met with the response "That's what he'd bloody get if he came in here!". No, the issue now was what we would call today "styling applications". To be specific, I should have subtitled this chapter "The Last Days of Brylcreem"! When I was becoming a teenager, haircreams and gels were absolutely "de rigueur" but my Dad would insist on putting the sodding stuff on me before we went out "in company", as it was known. February 1969 was the watershed when my views on this obnoxious practice finally prevailed and the wind could blow through my flowing locks all week, rather than being plastered down on Sundays or for major social events. Strange as it may seem, this was a pivotal moment in my personal development as I was able to throw off what had hitherto been a major parental shackle. It embodied the developing me; small but significant!

For the Dale, February began with a trip to play third-placed Lincoln City at Sincil Bank.

FEBRUARY 1969

Saturday 1st February
LINCOLN CITY 0 ROCHDALE 0
(Division 4)

Attendance: 8,681 Referee: Mr. K. Styles (Barnsley) H-T: 0-0

Harker
Smith   Parry   Ashworth   Ryder
Leech   Rudd
Whitehead   Melling   Jenkins   Butler

(Melledew as substitute replaced Melling after 50 minutes)

After four successive wins in which fifteen goals had been scored, the Dale went back into "mean and frugal" mode on their travels. The point gained owed much to Harker's bravery between the sticks and, once again, to Leech's inspirational qualities both in midfield and covering in defence, particularly in the last quarter of the game after Ashworth had been injured.

Major news stories during this week included the Palestine Liberation Organisation announcing the appointment of one Yasser Arafat as its leader. It is quite incredible, and somewhat depressing, that he occupies the same position today and all the same intrinsic and entrenched differences still exist between the Israelis and the Palestinians, despite efforts to achieve peaceful settlements or resolutions during the last thirty-three years. Indeed, the position seems to be worse than ever at the time of writing with a serious escalation in atrocities being committed on both sides. On a brighter note, this week also saw the maiden flight of the Boeing 747 Jumbo Jet, the largest commercial aircraft in the world. In the charts, "Blackberry Way" by The Move had replaced Fleetwood Mac at Number 1 but would last only one week before itself being replaced by "(If Paradise is) Half as Nice" by Amen Corner, the group fronted by Andy Fairweather-Low. As lead singer, he had an

ECHOES OF '69

unusual delivery style in that he did not appear to move, or even open, his mouth whilst singing, thus sharing a position with Keith Harris and Orville as the only chart-topping ventriloquist acts.

The Dale's next game should have been at home to Wrexham on Saturday 8th February but, as there was up to seven inches of snow lying on the Spotland pitch, the match was, naturally, postponed. This was the start of our half-term school holiday and, although we did not get a lot more snow, what had fallen remained on the ground as temperatures failed to rise above freezing for the whole week. I remember playing football every day with John, using the garage doors as goals as usual, but having the luxury of being able to perform diving saves and flying tipovers, safe in the knowledge of a snow-cushioned landing rather than rock-hard tarmac. It was magical (despite incipient frostbite in your extremities!). However, and for some inexplicable reason, the atrocious weather conditions had not impacted South Wales to the same extent and the game versus Newport County, originally postponed from 25th January, went ahead on the Monday night.

Monday 10th February
NEWPORT COUNTY 1 ROCHDALE 1
(Division 4)

Attendance: 2,607 Referee: Mr. B. Nicholls (Bournemouth) H-T: 1-1

Harker
Smith   Parry   Radcliffe   Ryder
Leech   Rudd
Whitehead   Melling   Jenkins   Butler
(Melledew was an unused substitute)

Despite the absence of the injured Ashworth, the Dale came back with their first point gained against a Welsh club this season (at the fifth attempt!) and extended the unbeaten run to six games.

FEBRUARY 1969

NEWPORT COUNTY A.F.C.

ROCHDALE

NEWPORT COUNTY

Vol. 3. No. 17. MONDAY, 10th FEBRUARY, 1969

President : Tom Jones
Vice-President : Syd Jenkins
Directors: Cyril Rogers (Chairman), H. C. Jones, Harry Morgan, J. F. Dymond, C. Howell

OFFICIAL PROGRAMME

INCLUDING FOOTBALL LEAGUE REVIEW

1/-

ECHOES OF '69

Some confusion exists over Newport's goal-scorer. I have variously seen it attributed to Tony Buck (of whom more soon), or a Vinny Leech own goal but, in the absence of a definitive ruling from Rothman's Football Yearbook (the statistician's bible) whose First Edition was published the following year covering season 1969-70, I will go with the Rochdale Observer's interpretation - sorry Vinny! Following this tenth minute setback, it took the Dale until the 44th minute to equalise when, from a corner, Jenkins headed against the crossbar for **Butler** to follow up the rebound and score. Following the game, Rochdale officials including manager Richley, stayed behind to negotiate the transfer of Tony Buck for a club record fee of £5,000, a move seen by Dale supporters as evidence of the Club's ambition to achieve promotion. Even Chairman Fred Ratcliffe was moved to comment that he felt Rochdale were "definite contenders for promotion" in justification of paying a fee of this size. Buck, at 5'11" and 11 stone, was a skilful centre-forward who had scored four goals in one game (albeit against poor old Bradford P.A) but further Arctic weather conditions would cause his debut for the Dale to be delayed.

During the following week, it was revealed that, for the first time, human eggs taken from female volunteers had been fertilised, in test-tubes, outside the womb. The disclosure came in a report published by Messrs. Edwards and Bavister of Cambridge University. What made it interesting from my personal perspective, however was that the research had been done in collaboration with Mr. Patrick Steptoe, the specialist in obstetrics and gynaecology at Boundary Park Hospital, Oldham. It was the very same Mr. Steptoe who had delivered me into the world some thirteen years earlier (my mum having sought specialist advice after sadly miscarrying in two pregnancies before me). At the time of the in-vitro fertilisation revelation, I would have undoubtedly kept quiet about this fact. After all, no self-respecting Dale fan would ever admit that he had been born at Boundary Park!

FEBRUARY 1969

Lingering snow from the previous week's storms meant that the game at Notts County, scheduled for Saturday 15th February, was postponed on the morning of the match but there was a busy day ahead anyway. In the late 60s, if there was one thing which you could rely on to take second place to football on a schoolboy's list of favourites, it was probably model trains. The Roche Valley Railway Society was holding its sixth annual model railway exhibition at Rochdale Fire Station that afternoon, so John and I duly turned up and spent a couple of hours looking at the various lay-outs which must have taken hours to set up. I had a small lay-out of my own permanently set up in my bedroom, an interest inculcated in me as a young child by my paternal grandfather who had been a train driver but, as my love of football grew, so my interest in model trains waned. I would eventually sell the complete set to Tommy Monaghan, father of neighbour and school friend Julie, who told me he was buying it for his grandchildren. His cover was blown a couple of months later, however, when I saw his wife and asked how he was doing with his lay-out. She told me that she never saw him as he had converted the loft and one of the bedrooms to accommodate the train set and, on one occasion, had shouted to him that his tea was ready, only to receive the reply that he couldn't come down because the 5:15 was due!

Incongruously, the next item on the day's agenda was my birthday party (I would reach thirteen the following day). In effect, you could say that I matured within the space of about six hours as I went from boys playing with toys (trains) to boys playing with dolls (except these were real ones). The guest list comprised, in the Blue corner, the boys; John Buckley, Derek Harvey, Terry Crabtree, John Nixon and myself. The Pink corner consisted of most of the best-looking (and certainly most well-developed) girls that class 3A1 could provide, namely; Beverley McKay, Susan Lowe, Christine Bentley and Barbara Pollard. You have to bear in mind that, although I was just thirteen, most

ECHOES OF '69

of these young ladies were already fourteen and that's a big difference in many respects! I will spare the reader any overly-graphic details but suffice to say that an enthusiastic game of "spin-the-bottle", with attendant serious snogging, soon broke out in my parents' darkened lounge, and it is for this reason that I will always associate Notts County (away-postponed) with "trapping-off" with Bev McKay! In later years, as part of my degree course and subsequent accountancy training, I would come to realise that statistics are like mini-skirts; they generate plenty of good ideas but hide the important things.

The big freeze continued in the North-West, indeed the following week brought fresh snowfalls and severe gales. One of Rochdale's main arterial roads, Kingsway, was blocked by drifting snow and the Observer carried pictures of drifts fifteen feet deep in Whitworth (which, to be fair, is above the permafrost line even in Summer!). A party of twenty-three kids from Redbrook High School, returning from a trip to London, were trapped for four hours on a coach on Saddleworth Moor by high winds and drifting snow (this was in the days before the M62, of course). They eventually found solace in the Clarence Hotel at Greenfield before being ferried home in police cars, which is actually exactly the kind of excitement you crave when you are in that 12-14 age group. A number of these kids would turn out to be future classmates of mine when I moved to Greenhill Upper School in the following September.

Despite the inclement weather, the club worked miracles to get the pitch playable for the following Saturday's scheduled game against promotion rivals Halifax Town, but the efforts were all in vain as the Yorkshire club cried off on the Friday as they had only eight fit players available. Over the weekend a further hardy band of some seventy volunteers helped to clear further snowfalls to enable the Monday night game to go ahead.

FEBRUARY 1969

Monday 24th February
ROCHDALE 2 DARLINGTON 0
(Division 4)

Attendance: 3,815 Referee: Mr. L. Cussons (York) H-T: 1-0

Harker
Smith   Parry   Ashworth   Ryder
Leech   Rudd
Whitehead   Buck   Jenkins   Butler
(Melling was an unused substitute)

As I mentioned in my introduction, this was the team formation that I will always associate with the Dale's historic season (although this could be seen as rather hard on "Whipp & Bourne's finest", Stevie Melledew, who would be "honorary sub"). It was record signing Tony Buck's debut and Darlington, who were hot favourites for promotion at this stage in the season, came into the game top of the table and, incredibly, still unbeaten away from home. In the 21st minute, the Quakers had a goal disallowed for offside and, within 30 seconds, Dale had scored. Whitehead pulled the ball back from the by-line, the keeper could only palm the ball to the edge of the box and **Jenkins** side-footed through the crowded area to score inside the post. Into the second half and Butler had his shot blocked, but **Jenkins** was again in the right place at the right time to tuck the ball home. Although he had failed to score, we were very impressed with Buck's contribution and as we trudged home through the snow, John and I agreed that we were in with a great chance of promotion. The team were now unbeaten in seven games and the result moved Rochdale up to ninth place in the table as February, mercifully, drew to a slightly warmer (maybe 5 or 6 degrees!) conclusion. The full table as at 28th February looked like this:

105

ECHOES OF '69

FOOTBALL LEAGUE DIVISION 4
February 28 1969

	P	W	D	L	F	A	Pts
Aldershot	29	16	5	8	50	32	37
Darlington	27	12	11	4	36	21	35
Chester	30	13	9	8	55	37	35
Colchester United	28	15	5	8	43	34	35
Doncaster Rovers	29	13	9	7	40	33	35
Workington	29	11	12	6	27	18	34
Lincoln City	30	12	10	8	36	32	34
Bradford City	29	11	11	7	41	32	33
ROCHDALE	**29**	**9**	**14**	**6**	**43**	**24**	**32**
Southend United	28	12	7	9	44	36	31
Brentford	29	10	10	9	44	33	30
Halifax Town	26	11	8	7	31	27	30
Scunthorpe United	29	11	6	12	40	41	28
Swansea Town	29	10	8	11	27	31	28
Newport County	32	8	12	12	37	48	28
Port Vale	28	9	9	10	30	28	27
Wrexham	27	9	8	10	38	27	26
Peterborough United	30	6	13	11	38	39	25
Chesterfield	28	8	9	12	39	36	25
York City	27	7	10	10	27	44	24
Notts County	29	7	9	13	31	45	23
Exeter City	29	7	8	14	40	49	22
Grimsby Town	30	6	9	15	35	50	21
Bradford Park Avenue	30	3	8	19	25	72	14

10.

MARCH 1969

Age does not make us childish, as men tell,
It merely finds us children still at heart.
Goethe, *Faust part 1* (1808)

March had arrived and Rochdale still had seventeen games to fulfil before mid-May when the season was scheduled to end. We were going to be busy!

Saturday 1st March
SCUNTHORPE UNITED 0 ROCHDALE 0
(Division 4)

Attendance: 3,044 Referee: Mr. V. Batty (Elsby) H-T: 0-0

Harker
Smith **Radcliffe** **Ashworth** **Ryder**
Leech **Rudd**
Whitehead **Buck** **Melling** **Butler**
(Melledew was an unused substitute)

The Dale were deprived of the services of both Parry and Jenkins for this game. Jenkins had the 'flu whilst Parry's poisoned leg caused him to miss his only game of the season. This dull draw was Rochdale's fifteenth out of their thirty league games to date and left them in ninth position in the table. Interestingly, Scunthorpe's line-up included a very young Kevin Keegan who had recently broken into the first team.

ECHOES OF '69

Rochdale's season was not the only thing taking off (cue another tenuous link!). The following day, Sunday 2nd, saw the maiden flight of the French Concorde from Toulouse; the UK version, Concord without the "e" originally, would not make its inaugural flight for another five weeks. Stranger still, the next edition of the Rochdale Observer ran a front page story that the Dale were considering flying to their upcoming match at Exeter and that twenty-four supporters were needed to fill the charter plane at £11 each. Unfortunately, this idea was later abandoned when it was discovered that, in the event of bad weather, charter flights out of Manchester Ringway were "put to the back of the queue" by air-traffic control. Also going up this week was the Rochdale College of Art on Fleece Street - unfortunately, it went up in flames!

Saturday 8th March
ROCHDALE 4 COLCHESTER UNITED 0
(Division 4)

Attendance: 4,988 Referee: Mr. J. Thacker (Scarborough) H-T: 0-0

Harker
Smith   Parry   Ashworth   Ryder
Leech   Rudd
Whitehead   Buck   Jenkins   Butler
(Melling was an unused substitute)

After a goalless first-half, during which Butler had hit the inside of the post with a shot from 20 yards, the game sprang to life against a Colchester team which had started the day in third position. The second half goal-fest began on 51 minutes when **Jenkins** flicked a long ball from Smith over the advancing goalie. Then, after intercepting a misplaced backpass in the 75th minute, **Butler** found the net at the second attempt as the 'keeper blocked his first effort. There followed the moment that the crowd (or at least the Dale

MARCH 1969

proportion thereof, which was nearly 100%) had been waiting for, when Tony Buck opened his account for the club. On 82 minutes the referee played advantage when Butler was clearly fouled inside the area and **Buck** drove the ball home from an acute angle. The rout was completed in the 90th minute when Rudd and Jenkins combined to send in **Butler** to score his second with ease against a now dispirited Colchester defence. What a win! And what a boisterous band of brothers we were as we wended our weary way home (Mr. Tinkler taught me that this is alliteration!) down Wilbutts Lane and along Spotland Road, looking forward excitedly to Monday night's game and asking ourselves how long this unbeaten run could last?

Monday 10th March
ROCHDALE 2 LINCOLN CITY 1
(Division 4)

Attendance: 5,003 Referee: Mr. V. James (York) H-T: 1-1

Harker
Smith   Parry   Ashworth   Ryder
Leech   Rudd
Whitehead   Buck   Jenkins   Butler
(Melledew was an unused substitute)

The answer was that the run would extend by another game and had now reached double figures. Ten games without defeat and seven of those had ended in victory! These were heady days indeed, and the Rochdale paying public were beginning to respond as the club recorded its first 5,000+ attendance of the season. This was another match versus opposition who were above the Dale in the table and had their own promotion aspirations. It was a considerably more difficult game than the Saturday previous as Lincoln battled hard but, after 30 minutes, the Dale took the lead when, following a

ECHOES OF '69

corner kick, the ball ran loose to **Butler** who blasted the ball home. However, Lincoln fought back and, right on half-time, Lewis burst through tackles by both Ryder and Smith to shoot past Harker. Not for the last time this season, the Dale showed their spirit and resilience by roaring back after the break and, just six minutes into the second half, the Lincoln 'keeper completely missed Whitehead's corner and **Buck** scored by virtue of simply chesting the ball into the empty net - unusual but, as they say, "they all count"! This victory took the Dale above Lincoln and into fifth place in the table.

The number one song in the pop charts by this time was "Where Do You Go To My Lovely" by Peter Sarstedt, but by far the biggest news item came on 12th March when Paul McCartney broke the hearts of girls, young and old, the length and breadth of the country (and overseas no doubt), when he married Linda Eastman. Not to be outdone, eight days later John Lennon and Yoko Ono got married in Gibraltar ("…near Spain, Christ you know it ain't easy"!). They then proceeded to spend most of the next week performing for a media circus in a so-called "bed-in" at the Amsterdam Hilton hotel - Lennon was of course in his hirsute, white suit phase during this period.

Still in the world of entertainment, appearing that week in March 1969 at that mecca of the club circuit, the Broadway Club in Failsworth, Manchester was the renowned Northern comedian, Al Read. This chap, a great favourite of my Dad's, specialised in rambling monologues which tended to the mildly risqué. He had a Sunday afternoon radio show which we used to tune into when we (the family) went out on Sunday afternoon drives. I'm sure that this was a much milder version than his club act and I recall the following example of his humour:

Read is tending to his garden when a four year old girl appears at the gate;

Little Girl; *"What are you doing Mister?"*
Al Read; *"I'm weeding."*
Little Girl; *"I weed!"*

MARCH 1969

Al Read (doubtfully); *"Do you really?"*
Little Girl; *"I weed in my chair!"*
Al Read; *"Oh, that's..."*
Little Girl carries on earnestly; *"Yes, I weed Wobinson Cwusoe in my chair!"*

This is a gentle piece of humour which has stuck in my memory over the years and I'm sure my Dad was expecting to hear Mr Read when we tuned in to a new programme on Sunday afternoon which was actually entitled "I'm Sorry, I'll Read That Again" (not, as my Dad mistakenly heard, "I'm sorry Al Read that again"!). This programme was revolutionary to my young ears and light years ahead of any previous radio comedy (even the fabulous "Round the Horne", which I loved). The cast consisted of various comic geniuses (genii?) who would ultimately become "Monty Python's Flying Circus" and "the Goodies" and I literally used to ache with laughter after each half-hour episode. This particular week, they carried a sketch of a Master of Ceremonies announcing the arrival of guests at a formal Ball who all had spoof names. I can only remember a few which went something like:

*Mr. and Mrs. **Biggun** and their son **Ivor**,*

*Mr. and Mrs. **Icklun** and their son **Ivan**,*

*Doctor and Mrs. **Sthesia** and their daughter **Annie**,*

*Mr. And Mrs. **Umming-Masser** and their son **Isaac**,*

Naturally, this was a major talking point at school the following day and some bright spark came up with the idea that we should submit a series of bogus applications to "Auntie Joyce" at the Rochdale Observer's "Young Readers' Club". Each edition of the paper carried a list of kids' names whose birthday fell around the date of that (bi-weekly) edition and, over the next five or six weeks, we

ECHOES OF '69

inundated their office with fictitious "children" such as:

Ivor Biggun and ***Ivan Icklun,***

Hugo First and ***Isobel Necessary,***

Hugh Jarse and ***Ian Continent,***

Lucy Lastic and ***Lou Stools,***

Ida Ninkling and ***Robin Banks,***

and my personal favourite, ***Norma Snockers!***

With a familiar nod to "Lanky dialect", we included:

Seth Issendown, Dusty Wantwan, Willie Eckerslike and ***Alf Hartagin.***

To show that we were becoming multi-racial and multi-cultural, we included a couple of Asians:

Mustapha Leek and (the cloakroom attendant) ***Mahatma Coat.***

Barry Lord, our resident boffin, had been swotting up on his biology textbooks and memorably came up with:

Polly Peptides.

Then, of course, matters descended to a cruder level (as they tend to do when you get a group of thirteen and fourteen year old lads together) and a joint application was submitted on behalf of the Scottish homosexuals:

MARCH 1969

Ben Doon and ***Phil McCafferty***

and their Irish counterparts:

Gerald Fitzwilliam and ***William Fitzgerald.***

I will draw a line under this episode but finish by admitting that, if I was doing this in the present day, I would have to include the Indian karaoke champion ***Gorrupta Singh!*** Sadly, I believe that the Observer must have rumbled what was going on because, during the course of my research, I could not find any evidence of a single one of our invented names appearing in the paper. Shame really, we put a lot of time and effort into it.

Back on the football front, there was more transfer activity but this time it was a player leaving the club. Terry Melling had evidently asked for a transfer when Tony Buck had been signed and he could not get even a place on the bench, so, after just 20 League appearances in which he scored 8 goals, he was off to Darlington for a small fee. At a personal level, I was not particularly sorry to see him go (as you might imagine) - it was a case of, to paraphrase the "Two Ronnies", "Goodnight from him and F*** off you T**t from me"!!!

Saturday 15th March
EXETER CITY 2 ROCHDALE 2
(Division 4)

Attendance: 4,061 Referee: Mr. D. Counsell (Blagdon) H-T: 1-1

Harker
Smith **Parry** Ashworth Ryder
Leech **Rudd**
Whitehead Buck Jenkins **Butler**
(Melledew was an unused substitute)

ECHOES OF '69

Having eventually made the long journey to Exeter by coach rather than 'plane, the Dale won a hard-earned point from a game where, unusually, they let slip a winning position. Rochdale had taken the lead in the 26th minute when a short cross from Whitehead was spectacularly volleyed in by **Buck,** only for Exeter to equalise on 40 minutes through Mitten. Two minutes into the second half and **Buck** was on target again, this time after playing a neat one-two with Whitehead. Ryder kicked a goal-bound effort off the line but the Dale had countless opportunities to add to the score and put the game beyond Exeter until, in the 85th minute, Binny took the ball around Harker to score the equaliser. As a result, Rochdale dropped a place to sixth in the table.

Over the weekend, a fresh series of Arctic gales wreaked havoc in the North of England, bringing down power cables and depositing a fresh layer of snow. Rochdale's re-arranged game at Halifax on Tuesday 18th was again postponed as the ground was covered in a mixture of snow, ice and water, and an extension to the season to a point after the traditional finale of the F.A. Cup final was now a probability rather than a possibility.

Besides the weather, other events making the news this month included the election of a 70 year-old grandmother, Golda Meir, as Prime Minister of Israel despite the opposition voiced by an ultra-religious group whose adherents advised Jewish men not to look upon "strange women"! In addition, the East-end gangland twins Ronnie and Reggie Kray were convicted of murder and sentenced to a minimum of 30 years imprisonment. I cannot hear the name Kray without thinking of the way they were later lampooned by the Monty Python team as "Doug and Dinsdale Piranah" - "Stig O' Tracey" was interviewed about why Dinsdale had nailed Stig's head to the floor:

Stig; *"Well he 'ad to do it didn'e? I mean to be fair, there was nothing else he could do.. I 'ad transgressed the unwritten law".*

Interviewer; *"What had you done?"*

Stig; *"Er... Well 'e never told me that. But 'e gave me 'is word*

MARCH 1969

EXETER CITY FOOTBALL CLUB

Saturday, 15th March, 1969

Fourth Division

EXETER CITY

Versus

ROCHDALE

Kick-off 3.00 p.m.

OFFICIAL PROGRAMME 9D Nº 1048

ECHOES OF '69

that it was the case, and that's good enough for me with old Dinsy! I mean, 'e didn't want to nail my 'ead to the floor, I had to insist. 'E wanted to let me off. There's nothing Dinsdale wouldn't do for you!" Absolutely Classic!

Saturday 22nd March
ROCHDALE 1 PORT VALE 0
(Division 4)

Attendance: 4,860 Referee: Mr. S. Kayley (Preston) H-T: 0-0

Harker
Smith   Parry   Ashworth   Ryder
Leech   Rudd
Whitehead   Buck   Jenkins   Butler
(Melledew was an unused substitute)

By Saturday the snow had receded sufficiently for the match not to be in doubt, but the game as a spectacle was ruined by the still-fierce winds and Spotland in those days did not offer many places where you could comfortably shelter! An extra layer of clothing was a minimum requirement and even the new fashion "must-have" for boys of my age, the ubiquitous snorkel-hooded parka coat with the bright orange lining, was no guarantee against frostbite. Incidentally, do you recall the awful smell that these coats gave off when "the rabbit fur" around the hood got wet? It was gruesome! The match itself was a tense affair as the weight of expectation from the spectators translated itself to the players, who were curiously diffident in view of their recent excellent form. The Dale dominated the first half hour and a volley from Buck struck the post but, this incident apart, there was no end product to the team's efforts and, as the match wore on, the display became more nervous and disjointed. Then, as we were resigning ourselves to the return of the nil-nil syndrome, Whitehead finally beat the offside trap that Vale

MARCH 1969

had been employing throughout the game and his cross was lashed home by **Butler** for the only goal of the game (after 83 minutes). After the initial cheers for the goal had subsided, in the Sandy Lane End you could hear a curious phenomenon as a couple of thousand people simultaneously exhaled a deep sigh of relief - phew! As we walked home after the game (quickly, to try and get some warmth back into our extremities) we acknowledged that the Dale had "crabbed" this one very fortuitously, but "a win was a win" and whilst we were still in sixth position, the three teams immediately above us were only a single point ahead and we had games in hand. It was looking good!

For the first time in four weeks, there was a change at the top of the charts with Peter Sarstedt finally being replaced by Marvin Gaye's "I Heard it Through the Grapevine", as the Motown Sound bandwagon began to gather pace. At school, the new Cinema Club held its inaugural meeting as we settled back in our flip-up seats in the plush lecture theatre to watch Hitchcock's "North by North-West", one afternoon after school, just before "breaking-up" for Easter. The film was fine but not nearly so memorable as the blasting received by one of the kids who kept fidgeting and managing to get parts of his head in the path of the beam of the projector. The voice of Mr. Rattigan, one of the teachers, boomed down from the back of the theatre *"Remain still, you cretinous clot!"*. You probably don't need me to tell you that English was his principal subject.

Saturday 29th March
PETERBOROUGH UNITED 0 ROCHDALE 1
(Division 4)

Attendance: 4,107 Referee: Mr. K. Burns (Dudley) H-T: 0-0

Harker

Smith   **Parry**   **Ashworth**   **Ryder**

ECHOES OF '69

Leech   **Rudd**
Whitehead   **Buck**   **Jenkins**   **Butler**
(Melledew as substitute replaced Buck after 80 minutes)

This was the Dale's seventh successive away game without defeat and equalled the post-war record of thirteen consecutive undefeated matches, which had been established in 1954. In an eventful game, the "Posh" 'keeper pulled off a string of first class saves in the opening half but Rochdale simply could not break through. However, after 52 minutes, **Buck** finally broke the deadlock with a fierce header into the net from Whitehead's corner kick. The game turned ugly in the last ten minutes as Buck was carried off after a bad tackle and Butler was, unusually, booked for dissent. Substitute Melledew extracted revenge on Buck's aggressor (or, to put it in more colloquial terms, he tw*tted Peterborough's centre-half, Wile!) and was sent off for his trouble. Nevertheless, the Dale held out and found themselves in fourth place, and a promotion spot, by five o' clock.

Sunday 30th March saw an historic event in Rochdale's policing history as virtually the whole force performed a ceremonial march from the Town Hall to the Parish Church, and then back again after a short religious service. This event was in celebration of the forthcoming amalgamation, which would occur with effect from 1st April (how unfortunate!), of the Rochdale Borough police with the Lancashire Constabulary, thereby ending 112 years of "local" policing. Naturally, my mother, sister and I went along to watch as my Dad was part of the march but I recall that, as well as the uniformed officers, the plain-clothes C.I.D. also paraded. Looking at the Rochdale Observer picture archives I was amazed to note that, even in the supposedly trendy days of 1969, they were all dressed in similar overcoats and trilby hats (although to be fair, it was a vile day with intermittent squally showers). It set me wondering, if a similar event were held today, would the undercover police officers have to parade in ski-masks or false beards? I'd ask my Dad but he'd probably just say I was **still** a daft pillock.

MARCH 1969

The wet weather took its toll on the Spotland pitch again. Monday night's scheduled game versus Southend United was postponed because of water-logging and would subsequently be re-arranged for 10th May as the last game of the season. The league positions at the end of March looked like this:

FOOTBALL LEAGUE DIVISION 4

	P	Pts	Max
Doncaster Rovers	38	48	64
Bradford City	36	43	63
Aldershot	38	43	59
ROCHDALE	**35**	**42**	**64**
Chester	38	41	57
Colchester United	36	41	61
Lincoln City	39	41	55
Darlington	34	39	63
Workington	36	39	59
Halifax Town	32	38	66
Swansea Town	37	38	56
Southend United	34	37	61

At this stage, the Dale still had a realistic chance of ending the season as champions; the month of April would prove to be pivotal.

11.

APRIL 1969

Do engine-drivers, I wonder, eternally wish they were small boys?
Flann O'Brien, *The Best of Myles* (1968)

The Easter programme of matches is usually a decisive period in football for deciding championship, promotion and relegation issues. However, in 1969, there was such a backlog of games and Divison 4 was so tight and competitive, that nothing was going to be finalised by the Easter games although they would have a critical bearing on events. Rochdale F.C. now faced a "run-in" of eleven games in thirty-five days which would shape their destiny, starting with a home game on Easter Saturday.

Saturday 5th April
ROCHDALE 2 YORK CITY 1
(Division 4)

Attendance: 6,908 Referee: Mr. R. Baker (Crewe) H-T: 0-1

Harker
Smith   Parry   Ashworth   Ryder
Leech   Rudd
Whitehead   Buck   Jenkins   Butler
(Melledew was an unused substitute)

Everything looked to be "going pear-shaped" by half-time in this game. The Dale hardly mustered a strike on goal throughout the forty-five minutes and had fallen behind to a well-taken goal by

APRIL 1969

McDougall after just nine minutes. This, incidentally, was the same Ted McDougall who (often in combination with Phil Boyer who also played for York in this game) would go on to score many goals for Bournemouth, including an incredible nine in one FA Cup game versus Margate in 1971, before failing to shine in a desperately-poor Manchester United side in the early Seventies. However, the second half was a transformation as, showing great resilience, the Dale bounced back and equalised on 62 minutes from a most unlikely source, as an airborne **Smith** clubbed the ball beyond the far post from Buck's lay-off. This was only his second goal for the club in over 100 appearances and was greeted with joyous disbelief by the majority of the bumper crowd. Then, just three minutes later, a back-header from **Buck** surprised the goalkeeper and crept into the net for what would prove to be the winner. We hardly had time to savour the heady delights of third place in the table before the next big game, against the league leaders, was upon us.

Monday 7th April
ROCHDALE 0 DONCASTER ROVERS 0
(Division 4)

Attendance: 12,647 Referee: Mr. K. Wynn (Wolverhampton) H-T: 0-0

Harker
Smith   Parry   Ashworth   Ryder
Leech   Rudd
Whitehead   Buck   Jenkins   Butler
(Melledew was an unused substitute)

Neither John or I had ever seen Spotland so full as the biggest crowd for fifteen years crammed in to see this clash. For the first time in our spectating memories, we were unable to change ends at half-time because of the sheer crush of numbers and consequently

ECHOES OF '69

had to watch a really quite drab game from a vantage point near the corner flag at the Pearl Street end. Doncaster undoubtedly came for a point with a defensive 5-3-2 formation which the Dale did not have the guile to break down. This was the first home point dropped in eight games and the first time that the Dale had failed to score at Spotland since the end of November. The record unbeaten run was extended to fifteen games but would unfortunately come to a shuddering halt the very next day.

Tuesday 8th April
CHESTER 2 ROCHDALE 1
(Division 4)

Attendance: 3,820 Referee: Mr. H. Williams (Sheffield) H-T: 1-0

Harker

Smith   Parry   Ashworth   Ryder

Leech   Rudd

Whitehead   Buck   Jenkins   Butler

(Melledew as substitute replaced Buck after 51 minutes)

Three games in four days took their toll on a tired Dale side which, with a tiny squad of players (only sixteen featured throughout the whole season) did not enjoy the luxury of a rotation system. A curiously unadventurous Chester side, considering they were the Division's leading scorers with 68 goals coming into this game, took the lead in the 18th minute when, picking up a rebound from 'keeper Harker, Provan snapped the ball into the empty net. They put the game beyond Rochdale when Dearden scored with a header after 85 minutes and so **Melledew's** tenth league goal of the season in the last minute, when he hooked home Butler's inswinging corner, was academic. Results elsewhere conspired to drop the Dale two places to fifth spot, although still with games in hand on the teams above them.

APRIL 1969

Headline-making news this week was the maiden flight of the UK version of Concorde, piloted by Brian Trubshaw and described by this worthy as a "wizard flight" (surely an anachronistic use of slang or banter more appropriate to the Spitfire or Hurricane). The plane was expected to be in service by 1974 and sales of over four hundred units were confidently expected before commercial hopes were dashed by American noise level restrictions. Hearing impairment also surfaced in the charts as Desmond Dekker and the Aces replaced Marvin Gaye at Number 1 with "The Israelites"; everyone at school was convinced that he was actually singing *"my ears are alight"* (which might have been a more appropriate song for the Crazy World of Arthur Brown really). This was the funniest "misheard lyric" that we had come across since hearing one of the kids in the schoolyard singing Herman's Hermits "She's a Must to Avoid" as *"she's a muscular boy"*!

Returning to school after the Easter holiday, the big breaking news in school was that we were going to put on a Play and it was going to be for public consumption (God help them!). Prior to Easter, in Mr Tinkler's English classes, we had messed about with "Androcles and the Lion" and I'd played the part of an effeminate Roman nobleman (thank you - I heard that crack about type-casting!). The role was crap but at least I got the chance to slap a teacher in the gob and get away with it! This, however, was not deemed a suitable vehicle for the vast ocean of thespian talent which was Howarth Cross! No, instead, we were going to perform "Toad of Toad Hall", the musical stage version of "Wind in the Willows" (that favourite of all devotees of Charades). No auditions as such were held; rather it was a selection process more usually associated with the eighteenth century Royal Navy, i.e. the Press Gang! I found myself cast in the role of "Chief Stoat", which I thought would be reasonably straightforward until somebody mentioned, quite casually, that there was a solo singing spot in the play for this character. Also, I would be required to disport myself, in the full gaze of the public, wearing a pair of green ribbed tights!

ECHOES OF '69

Oh no! Oh horror! Oh s**t! Look guys, I've got enough to worry about with the Dale's promotion effort without having this additional stress as well! But the die was cast; the trapdoor was shut; I was in it (up to my neck, and it was brown and smelly). The public performances were scheduled for the middle of May, so at least they would not clash with any of Rochdale's remaining matches.

Saturday 12th April
BRADFORD CITY 1 ROCHDALE 1
(Division 4)

Attendance: 9,449 Referee: Mr. Quinn (Middlesbrough) H-T: 0-0

Harker
Smith   Parry   Ashworth   Ryder
Leech   Rudd
Whitehead   Buck   Jenkins   Butler

(Melledew as substitute replaced Jenkins after 70 minutes)

By all accounts, this was an excellent match despite being played on a heavy and saturated pitch. Bradford took the lead in the 65th minute when Harker completely missed his kick to leave Ham with the easy tack of scoring into an open goal. However, in the 73rd minute, following his introduction as substitute, Melledew's header was cleared off the line but **Ashworth** was on hand to hammer the rebound into the roof of the net (his first goal for the club). Rochdale finished the stronger team, which was testimony to their fitness on this pudding of a pitch, but they were unable to score the extra goal which would have brought victory.

On Sunday 13th April we could, had we so chosen, have paid a visit to the Odeon Cinema to see the Jerry Allen Organ Show, but, sadly, we chose not to and I am consequently unable to report to the gentle reader exactly how mighty Jerry's organ was! The games

APRIL 1969

were coming thick and fast now and we only had to wait two days for the next, another pivotal confrontation with a fellow promotion contender.

Monday 14th April
ROCHDALE 4 CHESTER 1
(Division 4)

Attendance: 4,884 Referee: Mr. P. Partridge (Middlesbrough) H-T: 1-1

Harker
Smith   Parry   Ashworth   Ryder
Leech   Rudd
Whitehead   Buck   Melledew   Butler

(Jenkins was an unused substitute)

On a dismal wet and windy night, clearly reflected in the acutely disappointing attendance, Melledew was re-introduced to the starting line-up at Jenkins' expense. This was a game which the Dale simply had to win after two games without a victory, and they set about a good Chester side with great determination, and not a little flair, to earn both points and, at the same time, effectively bring to an end Chester's own promotion aspirations. **Buck** opened the scoring for the Dale on 32 minutes when he lashed in Butler's low corner but there was a setback when Talbot equalised in the 44th minute after a shot came back off the post. Into the second half and Rochdale, undeterred, attacked relentlessly and were rewarded when, after a neat combination between Leech and Butler, **Melledew** was on hand to slide the ball home. A third goal was inevitable and it duly arrived on 63 minutes. Melledew and Buck played a neat one-two, Melledew's shot was only partially stopped by the 'keeper and **Butler** followed up to force the ball in. By now Rochdale's football was irresistible and the goal of the night followed, in the 84th minute, when, running on to Rudd's through ball,

ECHOES OF '69

Butler blasted low into the bottom corner. The win took the Dale back up to third place and, with just six games remaining, the top of the table was very congested; anything could still happen, from winning the championship itself to missing out on promotion altogether. The tension around the town was palpable and the top part of the table tells you exactly why this was so;

FOOTBALL LEAGUE DIVISION 4
April 19, 1968

Top 9 only

	P	HOME					AWAY					Pts
		W	D	L	F	A	W	D	L	F	A	
Doncaster Rovers	43	12	7	2	40	16	7	9	6	20	21	54
Colchester United	41	12	6	2	30	15	8	3	10	25	33	49
ROCHDALE	**40**	**11**	**6**	**2**	**41**	**10**	**4**	**12**	**5**	**20**	**22**	**48**
Lincoln City	43	12	5	4	36	18	4	11	7	16	31	48
Bradford City	39	9	8	2	29	13	6	9	5	24	24	47
Darlington	39	10	5	4	33	17	6	9	5	22	19	46
Halifax Town	37	11	5	3	29	18	5	9	4	16	16	46
Southend United	39	13	3	5	46	21	3	9	6	21	28	44
Chester	42	11	4	6	41	23	4	9	8	30	36	43

Saturday 19th April
ROCHDALE 0 CHESTERFIELD 0
(Division 4)

Attendance: 7,669 Referee: Mr. P. Baldwin (Middlesbrough) H-T: 1-1

Harker
Smith　Parry　Ashworth　Ryder
Leech　Rudd
Whitehead　Buck　Melledew　Butler

(Jenkins as substitute replaced Whitehead after 80 minutes)

The occasion rather got to the Dale players in this match and, to be frank, they did not really "get out of second gear", although Humphreys, the Spireites 'keeper, made a number of outstanding

APRIL 1969

saves. Melledew had a goal disallowed, for no apparent reason, in the 39th minute but otherwise there were few incidents of note, despite Chesterfield having a couple of chances (and heart-stopping moments) late in the game when they might have stolen it. The unbeaten home run now extended to eleven games and we were still in the top four but it was all very jittery. Looking back at the match programme from this game, I was surprised to see the name of Neil Warnock amongst the Chesterfield squad. In the late Eighties, after qualifying as a podiatrist, Warnock turned to management and took Scarborough into the Football League. He subsequently managed Huddersfield, Oldham and Bury before returning to his roots at Sheffield United, where he is manager today. However, at each of his last three clubs, he left as a reviled figure and the clubs themselves appeared to be left for the worse after his departure (he had a curious habit of seemingly signing the same players to re-join him at his new club on increasingly lucrative contracts). I had seen the fans reaction to him when he was managing Oldham and, in the latter days, it was not pleasant, but it was only when he brought his Bury side to Huddersfield that I fully appreciated quite how much he was despised. During a break in play whilst a Bury player was receiving treatment, Warnock wandered out of the technical area and along the touchline near to where Greg and I were seated. A man of about 35 or 40 seated next to us, with a son of about Greg's age, obviously saw his opportunity to release years of pent-up frustration occasioned by Warnock's perceived mismanagement and got up out of his seat to confront Warnock. With his back to the crowd, he was completely oblivious to the approaching spectator who stood immediately behind him, separated only by three feet and an advertising hoarding, and bellowed at the top of his voice, *"WARNOCK! YOU'RE NOTHING BUT A F***ING CHIROPODIST!"*. Warnock, clearly startled, leapt about four feet in the air and rapidly scuttled back to the dug-out. The language may have been excessive, especially in front of kids, but it was one of the funniest things I have ever seen at a football match.

ECHOES OF '69

Contemporary events during this week included, finally after a series of technical problems, the maiden voyage of the cruise liner Queen Elizabeth II and the murderer of Bobby Kennedy, the Palestinian, Sirhan Sirhan, was sentenced to death in the gas chamber by a Los Angeles jury. Such "nominal symmetry" has always fascinated me. Today, the most famous incidence of the phenomenon is the Neville brothers' dad, Neville Neville but I have personally known a Robert Roberts and a Stephen Stevens. The stand-out candidate, however, would have to be a kid who was at Greenhill Upper School at the same as I was, who carried the name Dervish Dervish like a millstone around his neck. What can the parents be thinking of in a situation like this (or did the priest/vicar have a bad case of hiccoughs during the christening)?

Wednesday 23rd April
ROCHDALE 2 WREXHAM 1
(Division 4)

Attendance: 6,752 Referee: Mr. K. Howley (Billingham) H-T: 2-1

Harker
Smith   Parry   Radcliffe   Ryder
Leech   Rudd
Whitehead   Buck   Melledew   Butler

(Jenkins was an unused substitute)

An injury sustained by Ashworth was enough to keep him out of the side and enforced the first change in the line-up since 10th March, indeed the same twelve players had been on duty for the last ten games. Rochdale again started the game in diffident fashion but two goals in four minutes changed the whole complexion of the match. The deadlock was broken in the 28th minute when, following a dodgy Wrexham back-pass, **Buck** placed an exquisite lob over the 'keeper. There then followed one of those moments in a football match where,

APRIL 1969

as a spectator, you just know that everything is alright and that your team is destined to win. As the ball trickled over the Wrexham goal-line, we waited for the referee to award a corner kick but, to everyone's astonishment, he pointed to the spot! Penalty to the Dale! Never one to look a gift horse in the mouth, **Butler** quickly lashed home the spot kick (presumably before the ref could change his mind) and thereby broke a club record by becoming the highest scoring winger since the War with fifteen goals. The win lifted Rochdale to the vertigo-inducing heights of second position in the table and we now had our fingertips metaphorically on promotion.

On the following Saturday (26th April) there was no league programme as it was FA Cup Final day. This was fortunate for the Dale as Ashworth, Buck and Leech were all injured and would not have been fit for a Saturday game. Younger readers may be surprised to learn that, not only were Manchester City in the Final, but they also succeeded in winning the trophy! Curiously, the goalscorer in a drab 1-0 victory was a chap called Neil Young who would end his football league career playing for Rochdale in the mid-Seventies. I have a recollection of him playing wide on the left in a four-man attack alongside Crosby, Stills and Nash (or maybe I'm getting confused here)!

Monday 28th April
NOTTS COUNTY 1 ROCHDALE 1
(Division 4)

Attendance: 3,677 Referee: Mr. D. Pugh (Chester) H-T: 1-0

Harker
Smith   Parry   Radcliffe   Ryder
Leech   Rudd
Whitehead   Buck   Melledew   Butler

(Jenkins as substitute replaced Buck after 84 minutes)

129

ECHOES OF '69

After an indifferent season, County had enjoyed a reasonable run which had lifted them up the League to a position some six places off the bottom, but they provided Rochdale with one of their most testing games of the season. Smith was booked for an over-zealous tackle midway through the first half but then disaster struck. Notts took the lead in the 44th minute through Butlin and, try as they might, the Dale could not find an equaliser. Jenkins came on in place of Buck with six minutes to go and the Rochdale supporters in the small crowd must have thought that the cup of promotion was going to be dashed from their lips (which is a poetic way of saying that they were going to cock it up at the last minute!). Then, with barely three minutes to go, Melledew lobbed the ball, somewhat hopefully, into the area for **Jenkins** to volley home a quite sensational goal. The Rochdale fans must have gone home deliriously happy, even those whose coach was draughty and cold after a couple of windows were bricked on leaving the ground by fans (?) apparently wearing Forest colours.

Had I been aware of the result, I too would have been deliriously happy. As it was, I was just delirious, having been sent home from school during the course of the afternoon with nausea and a raging temperature. It transpired that I had contracted German Measles (Rubella) and so I was confined to home for the rest of the week. This caused some mild consternation at school, where we were due to have the first full dress rehearsal for "Toad of Toad Hall"(at least I wouldn't have to wear the tights just yet!), but it was as nothing compared to the hysteria in the Jones household when Dr. Burkhardt responded to my plaintive question by saying that "No, it would not be a good idea to go to Spotland tomorrow night"! Sadist! The Dale were going to play what was just about the biggest and most important game in their history and I would be reclining on the settee looking pale and wan (actually I was red-cheeked and sweaty, but pale and wan sounded a bit more dramatic!). It was bad enough my having missed each of the three games this season in which the Dale had stuck six up the opposition but to miss the

APRIL 1969

Halifax showdown was just too much to bear. I waited until the Doc had been shown to the front door and my Mum was out of the room, before I pulled the cushion tightly over my face. Before the reader jumps to the erroneous conclusion that I was attempting suicide by self-suffocation, let me clarify the reasons for the use of the cushion, which were two-fold (the reasons, not the cushions!). Firstly, it covered the tears that welled up in my eyes when realisation set in that I would miss the match. Secondly, it effectively muffled the stream of frustrated obscenities which then proceeded to issue from my mouth (which would have turned my mum's hair white had she been within earshot!). So the following night, I was compelled to stand leaning against the windowsill of our front room on Halifax Road, nose against the glass, looking out at the traffic jam which built up from about six o'clock, as what seemed like the whole population of Halifax came along the A58 on the way to Spotland for the 7:30 kick-off. What an absolute bummer!

Wednesday 30th April
ROCHDALE 1 HALIFAX TOWN 0
(Division 4)

Attendance: 13,266 Referee: Mr. G. Jones (Lancaster) H-T: 1-0

Harker
Smith   Parry   Radcliffe   Ryder
Leech   Rudd
Whitehead   Melledew   Jenkins   Butler
(Buck was an unused substitute)

In a pulsating game of missed chances, the biggest home gate of the season saw two very good sides slugging it out like characters in a Wild West saloon brawl. Within the first ten minutes, Harker made one save from a goal-bound effort that came off Ryder's head via the

ECHOES OF '69

post. Then, on 17 minutes, Melledew had a shot kicked off the line before Halifax again hit the post in the 26th minute. After 35 minutes came the game's decisive moment. Letting onto a bobbling ball, some twenty yards out from goal, **Butler** smashed a swerving shot past the 'keeper and in off the far post! To the Dale supporters packed into Spotland, the relief was palpable but the tension would continue through the second half as Rochdale clung on to their lead. After 55 minutes they were extremely fortunate when a clear penalty for handball against Parry was not given but, equally, Halifax had a let-off when, in the 70th minute, Whitehead's drive from twenty yards smacked against the bar. Finally, the referee's whistle blew to signal the end of the game and the spectators, in Rochdale's best gate since 1954, left knowing that the Dale now needed just one point from their two remaining games to ensure promotion.

Back at home I, of course, was blissfully unaware of events and developments at Spotland. In the absence of the invention of Ceefax (or even a special GMR radio commentary) in those days, all I could do was grimly hang on for the football results on News at Ten. I doubtless sat through Coronation Street (which number wife would Ken Barlow be on then?, if you'll pardon the expression!) and possibly some arty-farty "Play for Today" featuring kids of my age popping Purple Hearts. As the traffic backed up again on Halifax Road from about half past nine, this time travelling in the opposite direction, I strained in the gloom to discern the condition of the (presumably Halifax-supporting) occupants of the slow-moving or stationary vehicles. To no avail; I could not tell if they were happy (we'd lost) or sad (we'd won) or just so-so (a draw)! The words of the Beatles' new number one *"Get back! Get back! Get back to where you once belonged"* seemed an appropriate send-off to the Halifax fans but it would be a further, tortuous, three-quarters of an hour before I knew the result, courtesy of News at Ten's Reginald Bosanquet:

APRIL 1969

"ROCHDALE 1 HALIFAX TOWN 0"

What a relief! I was, however, still badly p***ed off at having missed the game, especially when I learned the size of the crowd and what a great game it had been. I was determined that nothing would keep me away from the final home game of the season against Southend United, a week on Saturday.

As April came to a close, the top of the Division Four table looked like this:

FOOTBALL LEAGUE DIVISION 4
April 30 1969

Top 7 only

	P	W	D	L	F	A	PTS
Doncaster Rovers	45	20	17	8	62	37	57
ROCHDALE	**44**	**17**	**20**	**7**	**65**	**34**	**54**
Halifax Town	44	19	16	9	52	37	54
Bradford City	45	17	20	8	62	45	54
Darlington	45	17	18	10	61	42	52
Colchester United	46	20	12	14	57	53	52
Southend United	44	19	13	12	77	54	51

Anything was still possible as an outcome; first place and the Championship could not be ruled out; second, third or fourth place and thereby promotion to Division Three was the most probable; but (BUT!) the Dale still had the potential to "snatch defeat from the jaws of victory" and finish outside the top four if they were to lose both remaining games! An away game at Halifax and the home game versus Southend were all that remained. In terms of stress and anxiety, singing solo and wearing green tights in public was, by comparison, going to be a piece of a cake!

12.

MAY 1969

And it's not for the sake of a ribboned coat,
Or the selfish hope of a season's fame,
But his captain's hand on his shoulder smote -
'Play up! Play up! And play the game!'
Henry Newbolt, *'Vitai Lampada'* (1897)

Given that I had succeeded in shrugging off the debilitating effects of my spell of German measles and had managed to avoid any contact with pregnant women (happily, something I eventually maintained until well into my mid-thirties, by various means!), I was allowed to return to school on the first Monday in May. Note that there was no such thing as a May Day Bank Holiday in those days (as a future boss of mine, whose personal politics placed him slightly to the right of Genghis Khan, would say, *"May Day is for European Socialist poofs! We should have a Bank Holiday for St. George's Day!"*) There was a sort of electrically charged tension around the whole place now, as a direct function of the twin events of the forthcoming Play (first public performance now just over a week away) and the Dale's two dates with destiny. Doncaster Rovers clinched the Division Four championship by beating Grimsby 3-1 but we shrugged that disappointment off, along with Len Richley's dismissal of a reported £20,000 bid for Norman Whitehead by Sheffield United as "a complete fabrication". The news that the Queen Elizabeth II had reached New York on her maiden voyage had no effect on us whatsoever. We did not blink an eye at news of Jimi Hendrix' arrest in Toronto for possession of heroin and we certainly were not remotely (!) interested in pictures

MAY 1969

of the surface of Venus being beamed back at us from the rather unfortunately-named Russian spacecraft, Venera 5! Unfortunately, I disgraced myself during the final dress rehearsal for the Play on the Wednesday evening. Having been lured into a stationery cupboard by an attractive young Stoat, Cheryl Bradley, I abused my position as Chief of that species by engaging her in a major "snog", a situation aggravated by a conveniently-timed power cut of some five minutes duration. Emerging from the dark cupboard, with our Stoat whisker make-up smeared beyond recognition was, in retrospect, probably something of a give-away and we were duly chastised by sundry harassed teachers!

Come the Thursday evening and Halifax Road once again assumed the status of a car park as thousands of Rochdalians made their way to Halifax for the return fixture. I might have "cracked it" insofar as attending night matches at Spotland went, but I was never going to get away with a midweek trip to an away match, not even the short distance to Halifax. Consequently I again endured a number of anxious hours before finding out the match result.

Thursday 8th May
HALIFAX TOWN 1 ROCHDALE 0
(Division 4)

Attendance: 17,188 Referee: Mr. J. Hunting (Leicester) H-T: 0-0

Harker
Smith   Parry   Ashworth   Ryder
Leech   Rudd
Whitehead   Melledew   Jenkins   Butler

(Buck as substitute replaced Rudd after 82 minutes)

The game was, once again, a hard-fought close encounter, played out before a massive crowd although, but for Harker's heroics in goal, Halifax might have been three-up at half-time. As it was, the

ECHOES OF '69

Dale held out until just fifteen minutes from time when Massie gave the Shaymen the lead. Despite substituting Buck for Rudd, Rochdale could not conjure up an equaliser and the game was lost. The result meant that Halifax were definitely promoted whilst the Dale still had to sweat it out.

The following night (Friday) saw Bradford City beat Darlington to clinch their own promotion and deny Darlo the opportunity to match the Dale's points total. This left the table in the following state:

FOOTBALL LEAGUE DIVISION 4
May 9 1969

Top 7 only

	P	W	D	L	F	A	PTS
Doncaster Rovers	46	21	17	8	65	38	59
Bradford City	46	18	20	8	65	46	56
Halifax Town	45	20	16	9	53	37	56
ROCHDALE	**45**	**17**	**20**	**8**	**65**	**35**	**54**
Darlington	46	17	18	11	62	45	52
Colchester United	46	20	12	14	57	53	52
Southend United	44	19	13	12	77	54	51

The mathematics were quite straightforward; merely a draw for the Dale the next day would see them promoted whilst a defeat would see them nervously biting their fingernails and awaiting the result of Southend's final game. The whole season had effectively come down to a single game of "sudden death" and it could not have been more dramatic.

I can recall sleeping only fitfully that night, whether by virtue of excitement or dread fear of losing the game, I'm not sure which. I got up early and read the Rochdale Observer from cover to cover and it was still only nine o'clock. The morning dragged on interminably, time seemingly standing still. I set up the Subbuteo pitch in my bedroom, smoothing out the lush green baize cloth and getting as far as laying my blue and white Rochdale team out in 4-2-4 formation

MAY 1969

when something made me stop. Was I tempting fate by having my miniature Dale annihilate a miniature Southend United? I didn't know but I wasn't going to take any chances with Providence, so away went the Subbuteo in double quick time! I got my books out with the intention of starting on my History homework essay but, within five minutes, these too had been put back away. I simply could not concentrate and I was reduced to a nervous wreck, pacing around the house like a caged tiger desperate to find something to occupy my mind. A cigarette or a stiff brandy might have worked but, sadly, these were not available options at age thirteen! Even the "Banana Splits" on TV failed to raise a smile and so, much to my parents' relief (who had been "walking on eggshells" all morning and trying to humour me), I decided to go and call for John early on the basis that a "problem shared is a problem halved" (or "a friend in need is a bloody nuisance"!). I found him in approximately the same state (i.e. "bricking it"), so we set off for the Town Centre with the intention of catching the bus up to the ground. The Spotland bus (were the buses still cream and blue or had we already changed to SELNEC orange?) was already in at its terminus (outside the Empire cinema, which may already have converted to bingo, and adjacent to the Flying Horse) with the engine running. The bus set off as we made our way up the open-platformed staircase (these were the days when a bus really was a bus!) and as we reached the top deck, there was one other passenger on board who was occupying the rear seat. John walked past the guy and sat down but I did a classic double-take and made a complete prat of myself as I banged my head on one of the safety grab-poles as I walked on and, at the same time, turned my head through about 180 degrees. I saw the guy smile wryly to himself as I sat down next to John and hissed *"Have you seen who's sitting there? It's only Colin Parry!"* (for verily t'was he!). Now fast forward thirty-three years and try to imagine a present day situation where two young lads on their way to the match find themselves on the same bus as one of their heroes. Pretty unlikely contingency, I would suggest. You have a far greater

ECHOES OF '69

chance of being run over by Teddy Sheringham's Ferrari or Beckham's Aston Martin! So, back on the Spotland bus in 1969, John and I agonised in hushed tones about whether or not we should speak to the great man, awestruck as we were. After deciding that we **should** exchange pleasantries, we then had a two minute interlude of, *"Go on then. You say something!", "No, I don't know what to say. You say something!"* before I uttered the immortal words ***"Are you going to the match then Mr. Parry?"***!!! I immediately wanted to curl up and die! What a bloody stupid question, moron! Where else could he be going? Displaying commendable tact and diplomacy, Colin Parry replied that he was indeed going to the match and would we be cheering the Dale on to promotion? (What a good job it wasn't Melling that we had bumped into! I shudder to think what his response might have been). The upshot was that we had a very pleasant conversation with one of our heroes but, typically, I could not get through the experience without making a complete pillock of myself (my Dad was obviously spot-on in that respect!). An old guy got on the bus and, as soon as he sat down, lit up his pipe. Clouds of noxious fumes drifted towards the back seats and Colin Parry's nose curled up in distaste. Without stopping to think of the consequences, I launched into a little monologue containing a conversation I had overheard my Dad have with one of his fellow officers down at Rochdale "nick". My Dad, himself an occasional pipe-smoker, had lit up one day and his colleague asked him what tobacco he was using. When my dad replied "Three Nuns", his colleague's riposte was "Well then, one of them must have shit herself!". As I looked at John covering his head with his hands, I realised that this was probably not the most appropriate piece of repartee I could have come up with in the circumstances and the old boy had turned around to look daggers at me. Parry merely smiled, indulgently, and we shook hands with him as we got off the bus before letting him stride off on his own up Wilbutts Lane. John was obviously of the same opinion as my Dad; he just looked up and down at me and said, simply "You Pillock!".

MAY 1969

There were still two hours to go before kick-off, so we hung around waiting for the turnstiles to be opened. Already there were lots of people milling around outside the ground and we decided that our strategy would be to gain entry as early as possible, find a spot in the Sandy Lane End and stay there, fully expecting a large turnout from the Rochdale public. At approximately 1:30, the first turnstile opened. We paid our admission and dashed to the middle of the Sandy, and in a completely empty stadium, staked our place leaning on the wall immediately behind the nets. Over the course of the next hour and a half, as the ground filled up, we would have to repel a few boarders and claim-jumpers to our spot but, as the teams filed out just before three o' clock, we were in place to cheer on our team to the most important ninety minutes in the club's history.

Saturday 10th May
ROCHDALE 3 SOUTHEND UNITED 0
(Division 4)

Attendance: 9,095 Referee: Mr. R. Tinkler (Boston) H-T: 1-0

Harker

Smith   Parry   Ashworth   Ryder

Leech   Rudd

Whitehead   Melledew   Jenkins   Butler

(Buck as substitute replaced Rudd after 82 minutes)

If the spectators' anxiety had been manifested at some of the more recent home games, it was nothing compared to the atmosphere at this match as the sheer tension engendered by the occasion crackled around the terraces like an electrical storm (or Barry Lord with the Van Der Graaf Generator!). Fingernails were being bitten to the quick and, with Rochdale attacking the opposite Pearl Street end in the first half and spectators striving to get a clear view, the Sandy was a sea of bobbing heads and craning necks more reminiscent of a rave party for mating swans! From our vantage point behind the goal we were fine, if somewhat low down and suffering a restricted perspective, so long as Chris Harker kept moving around. Then, in the 15th minute, some of the crowd's anxiety was allayed as **Melledew** got his strike on goal. A defender managed to clear the ball but, to our immense relief, referee Tinkler ruled that the ball had crossed the line. GOAL! One-up to the Dale! Again you felt that this pivotal moment was part of the season's destiny, it **was** going to happen, promotion **was** going to be won, and some of the spark seemed to go out of Southend following this setback to their hopes. Throughout the rest of the half we cheered as Dale defenders hoofed the ball into touch or made clean tackles, and clapped like demented seals whenever Harker made a save, or just collected the ball. Repeated nervous glances at the wristwatch confirmed that time really **had** slowed down, five minutes actual time elapsing for every minute that ticked off the watch, or so it seemed but, eventually, the referee signalled for half-time to a chorus of a huge sigh of relief and puffing out of cheeks. We were half-way there but still not prepared to take anything for granted.

The second half kicked off to a huge roar and, each time that Rochdale gained possession, the Sandy Lane crowd almost seemed to be trying to suck the ball towards the goal. The tension rose to almost unbearable heights and I was literally shaking with excitement and nervous energy, kicking every ball and jumping for every header, hurling undeserved abuse at Southend's defenders and 'keeper. After 55 minutes nerves were pulled as taut as a bow-string when, from Rudd's pinpoint cross, Melledew contrived to put his header onto the crossbar, and out for a goal-kick, when it looked easier to score than to miss. But cometh the hour (or to be precise, cometh the 67th minute), cometh the man and

MAY 1969

that man was the crowd's real hero - "Big Reg" Jenkins. Billy Rudd, not for the first time this season, was brought down in the box and, if the ref was not immediately convinced that it was a foul, then half a second later he certainly was as 9,000 voices bellowed **"PENALTY!!!"** in unison. **Jenkins** placed the ball, walked back about five paces, turned and, almost casually, smashed the ball past the 'keeper and into the net! The roof almost came off the Sandy, such was the decibel rating of the tremendous cheer that went up. Everybody around me was jigging around, embracing and hugging their neighbour or falling over to be semi-trampled by a wave of bodies tumbling down the tightly packed terrace. It might have seemed dangerous to the casual onlooker but there weren't any casual onlookers there! - just demented and semi-deranged Dale fans who realised that, at 2-0 up, with only a quarter of the game remaining, the tension and anxiety could be shelved and that the rest of the match was there to be enjoyed. We clamoured for another goal to settle the game and the team did not disappoint us. On 80 minutes, Smith got to the by-line and pulled the ball back to **Jenkins,** standing right in front of John and I on the 6-yard line, who thumped the ball right-footed into the net! Again the crowd went wild, but this time in the absolutely certain knowledge that we had won and we were going up. After 85 minutes Rudd was substituted, to deafening applause, to allow Tony Buck to share the spotlight, but by now the crowd, young and old alike, were jockeying for position to get over the fence and get to their heroes at the final whistle. A small cordon of policemen began to take up position along the touchlines but they had as much hope of success as King Canute had of holding back the tide - at best they could delay the flood of adoring fans sufficiently to enable the team to escape to the safety of the dressing room, or so they thought. In fact they were wrong! As the referee blew his whistle, it was like the starting pistol for the Olympic 100 metres final but with 9,000 competitors. Most of the team did not manage to reach the half-way point to the tunnel before they were engulfed in a whooping sea of blue and white. From my vantage point on the touch-line wall, I got a flying start, neatly side-stepped a burly constable and succeeded in slapping Norman Whitehead on the back (as right-winger he probably had the greatest distance to cover before finding sanctuary). However, that was about as far as I got before being bowled over in the rush and trampled what felt like three feet down in the Spotland turf and mud! As John helped me back onto my feet, shaken but undeterred, we joined the throng gathering in front of the Main Stand and joined in the chanting:

"We're going up! We're going up! Ee-aye-addio we're going up!"

Then the crowd clamoured for their heroes to make an appearance and receive the acclamation of their supporters as we shouted:

"Bring 'em out!" and *"We want Len!"*

One by one, the players appeared in the Stand to rapturous applause and then, in a nice touch, themselves applauded the arrival of manager Len Richley and Chairman Fred Ratcliffe. Poor old Fred! Having achieved one of his life's ambitions, and with tears of true joy in his eyes, he was asked to say a few words but found the occasion too much for him, the Observer later reporting that all he could say was "I can't speak!". As the players disappeared back to the dressing room, the crowd's last cheer was reserved for Stevie Melledew who, possibly thinking back to the short time since he had been playing as an amateur for Whipp and Bourne's works team, gave the Rochdale public an emotional clenched fist salute to send us on our way. As I walked home, still giddy from the heady excitement of the day, I gave only a fleeting thought to the emotional salute that my mum was likely to give **me** when she saw the muddied state of my Sea Dogs and Parka! Who cares? It was worth it!

13.

AFTERMATH

Success is counted sweetest
By those who ne'er succeed,
To comprehend a nectar
Requires sorest need.
  Emily Dickinson (1859)

As soon as promotion was confirmed they all came out of the woodwork! The "fans for forty years" and "lifelong fans now exiled in Plymouth/Inverness/Sydney", you name it, they wrote in their dozens to the Observer. They "never had a doubt" that the Dale would be promoted and had "supported them through thick and thin". Almost as vomit-inducing were the business advertisements placed in the newspaper "congratulating the Dale on their promotion" although most of them had probably stuck up a metaphorical two fingers when they had been approached to place an ad in the match programme earlier in the season. One of the most curious (petty?) came from Bradley's Music, Drake Street, Rochdale, who alongside the congratulatory verbiage also included the extraordinary:

"We installed the public address system and supplied the organ for the Social Club"!!!

As I wrote this, the most awful realisation suddenly hit me. The Bradley in question was, it all comes back to me now, the father of the attractive young Stoat with whom I had the Stationery cupboard encounter!

ECHOES OF '69

THE SEASON MATCH BY MATCH

Rochdale Observer, Wednesday 21 May 1969 — Reproduced by the Rochdale Observer from the Souvenir Edition of 14th May 1969

THE struggle lasted from August 1968 to May 1969 covered 46 games, 4,140 minutes of football. At the end Rochdale had 56 points—enough to take them into the Third Division. Here is the match-by-match record of those games.

And then the champagne. Chairman F S Ratcliffe joins his players in the dressing room to toast their success and to thank them for bringing him this day for which he's waited 17 years.

From the directors' box the heroes after their applause to chairman, manager Len Richley and trainer-coach Dick Conner.

ROCHDALE 3
SCUNTHORPE UNITED 2
Harker; Radcliffe, Ryder, Leech, Parry, Ashworth, Whitehead, Fletcher, Jenkins, Rudd, Butler; Sub: Riley. Scorers: Jenkins (two penalties), Butler. Attendance: 2,193.

COLCHESTER UNITED 0
ROCHDALE 0
Harker; Radcliffe, Ryder, Leech, Parry, Ashworth, Whitehead, Melledew, Jenkins, Rudd, Butler; Sub: Fletcher for Whitehead, injured, 75 minutes.

ROCHDALE 2
EXETER CITY 1
Harker; Radcliffe, Ryder, Leech, Parry, Ashworth, Whitehead, Melledew, Jenkins, Rudd, Butler; Sub: Fletcher. Scorers: Melledew. Attendance: 2,325.

BRENTFORD 2
ROCHDALE 1
Harker; Radcliffe, Ryder, Leech, Parry, Ashworth, Whitehead, Melledew, Jenkins, Rudd, Butler; Sub: Smith, for Butler, 60 minutes. Scorer: Melledew.

PORT VALE 2
ROCHDALE 1
Harker; Radcliffe, Ryder, Leech, Parry, Smith, Whitehead, Melledew, Jenkins, Ashworth, Rudd; Sub: Butler, for Whitehead, 83 minutes. Scorer: Melledew.

ROCHDALE 4
PETERBOROUGH UTD 1
Harker; Radcliffe, Ryder, Leech, Parry, Ashworth, Whitehead, Melledew, Jenkins, Rudd, Butler; Sub: Fletcher, for Butler, 70 minutes. Scorer: Melledew. Attendance: 4,639.

CHESTERFIELD 1
ROCHDALE 0
Harker; Radcliffe, Ryder, Leech, Parry, Ashworth, Fletcher, Melledew, Jenkins, Rudd, Butler; Sub: Whitehead, for Jenkins, 75 minutes. Scorer: Melledew.

DONCASTER ROVERS 2
ROCHDALE 0
Harker; Radcliffe, Ryder, Leech, Parry, Ashworth, Riley, Melledew, Fletcher, Rudd, Butler; Sub: Jenkins.

ROCHDALE 1
BRADFORD CITY 1
Harker; Radcliffe, Ryder, Leech, Parry, Ashworth, Fletcher, Butler, Smith, Rudd, Riley; Scorer: Fletcher (2), Melledew (2), Rudd. Butler. Attendance: 4,118.

YORK CITY 0
ROCHDALE 0
Harker; Radcliffe, Ryder, Leech, Parry, Ashworth, Fletcher, Melledew, Melling, Rudd, Butler; Sub: Whitehead.

ROCHDALE 0
WORKINGTON TOWN 0
Harker; Radcliffe, Ryder, Leech, Parry, Ashworth, Fletcher, Melledew, Melling, Rudd, Butler; Sub: Jenkins, for Fletcher, 62 minutes. Attendance: 4,565.

ROCHDALE 0
NOTTS COUNTY 0
Harker; Radcliffe, Ryder, Smith, Parry, Ashworth, Whitehead, Fletcher, Melling, Rudd, Butler; Sub: Melledew, for Butler, 90 minutes. Attendance: 7,872.

ROCHDALE 0
BRADFORD 0
Harker; Radcliffe, Ryder, Leech, Parry, Smith, Whitehead, Melledew, Melling, Rudd, Butler; Sub: Jenkins. Scorers: Rudd (2) penalty). Butler. Melledew. Melling. Radcliffe. Attendance: 2,705.

ROCHDALE 1
NEWPORT COUNTY 1
Harker; Radcliffe, Ryder, Smith, Parry, Ashworth, Whitehead, Rudd, Melling, Jenkins, Butler; Sub: Jenkins, for Melling. Attendance: 4,222.

ALDERSHOT 3
ROCHDALE 0
Harker; Radcliffe, Ryder, Leech, Parry, Ashworth, Whitehead, Melledew, Melling, Rudd, Butler; Sub: Fletcher.

ROCHDALE 0
WREXHAM 3
Harker; Radcliffe, Ryder, Leech, Parry, Ashworth, Whitehead, Melledew, Melling, Rudd, Butler; Sub: Smith. Scorer: Melling (2).

SWANSEA TOWN 3
ROCHDALE 1
Harker; Radcliffe, Ryder, Leech, Parry, Ashworth, Whitehead, Rudd, Melling, Jenkins, Butler; Sub: Melledew.

WORKINGTON TOWN 1
ROCHDALE 1
Harker; Smith, Ryder, Leech, Parry, Ashworth, Whitehead, Rudd, Melling, Jenkins, Butler; Sub: Melledew. Scorer: Butler (2), Jenkins, Buck. Attendance: 2,038.

BRADFORD 0
ROCHDALE 1
Harker; Smith, Ryder, Leech, Parry, Ashworth, Whitehead, Rudd, Melling, Jenkins, Butler; Sub: Buck, Riley. Scorers: Melling (2), Whitehead.

ROCHDALE 2
ALDERSHOT 0
Harker; Smith, Ryder, Leech, Pacey, Ashworth, Whitehead, Rudd, Melling, Melledew, Butler; Sub: Riley. Scorer: Butler (2), Melling. Attendance: 3,362.

LINCOLN CITY 1
ROCHDALE 0
Harker; Smith, Ryder, Leech, Parry, Ashworth, Whitehead, Rudd, Melling, Jenkins, Butler; Sub: Melledew. Scorer: Butler.

NEWPORT COUNTY 1
ROCHDALE 1
Harker; Smith, Ryder, Leech, Parry, Radcliffe, Whitehead, Rudd, Melling, Jenkins, Butler; Sub: Melledew. Scorer: Buck, Smith. Attendance: 6,960.

ROCHDALE 0
DARLINGTON 0
Harker; Smith, Ryder, Leech, Parry, Ashworth, Whitehead, Rudd, Buck, Jenkins, Butler; Sub: Melling. Scorer: Jenkins (2). Attendance: 2,815.

SCUNTHORPE UNITED 0
ROCHDALE 0
Harker; Smith, Ashworth, Whitehead, Radcliffe, Ashworth, Whitehead, Rudd, Buck, Melling, Butler; Sub: Jenkins. Scorer: Butler. Attendance: 4,291.

ROCHDALE 0
COLCHESTER UNITED 0
Harker; Smith, Ryder, Leech, Parry, Ashworth, Whitehead, Rudd, Buck, Jenkins, Butler; Sub: Melling. Scorer: Butler (2), Jenkins, Buck. Attendance: 4,680.

ROCHDALE 0
LINCOLN CITY 1
Harker; Smith, Ryder, Leech, Parry, Ashworth, Whitehead, Rudd, Buck, Jenkins, Butler; Sub: Melledew. Scorer: Butler, Attendance: 3,900.

EXETER CITY 0
ROCHDALE 0
Harker; Smith, Ryder, Leech, Parry, Ashworth, Whitehead, Rudd, Buck, Jenkins, Butler; Scorer: Buck (2).

ROCHDALE 2
PORT VALE 0
Harker; Smith, Ryder, Leech, Parry, Ashworth, Whitehead, Rudd, Buck, Jenkins, Butler; Sub: Melledew. Scorer: Butler. Attendance: 4,280.

PETERBOROUGH UTD 0
ROCHDALE 0
Harker; Smith, Ryder, Leech, Parry, Ashworth, Whitehead, Rudd, Buck, Melling, Butler; Sub: Melledew, for Buck, injured, 50 minutes. Scorer: Buck.

ROCHDALE 4
CHESTER 0
Harker; Smith, Ryder, Leech, Parry, Ashworth, Whitehead, Rudd, Buck, Melledew, Butler; Sub: Jenkins. Scorers: Butler, 2, Buck, Melledew. Attendance: 4,881.

ROCHDALE 0
CHESTERFIELD 0
Harker; Smith, Ryder, Leech, Parry, Ashworth, Whitehead, Rudd, Buck, Melledew, Butler; Sub: Jenkins, for Whitehead, 50 minutes. Attendance: 7,968.

ROCHDALE 1
WREXHAM 0
Harker; Smith, Ryder, Leech, Parry, Ashworth, Whitehead, Rudd, Buck, Melledew, Butler; Sub: Jenkins. Scorers: Buck, Butler (penalty). Attendance: 6,735.

NOTTS COUNTY 1
ROCHDALE 1
Harker; Smith, Ryder, Leech, Parry, Radcliffe, Whitehead, Rudd, Buck, Melledew, Butler; Sub: Jenkins, for Buck, injured, 84 minutes. Scorer: Jenkins.

ROCHDALE 0
HALIFAX TOWN 0
Harker; Smith, Ryder, Leech, Parry, Radcliffe, Whitehead, Rudd, Melledew, Jenkins, Butler; Sub: Buck. Scorer: Butler. Attendance: 13,266.

HALIFAX TOWN 1
ROCHDALE 1
Harker; Smith, Ryder, Leech, Parry, Ashworth, Whitehead, Rudd, Melledew, Jenkins, Butler; Sub: Buck, for Rudd, 80 minutes. Attendance: 17,168.

ROCHDALE 1
SOUTHEND UNITED 0
Harker; Smith, Ryder, Leech, Parry, Ashworth, Whitehead, Rudd, Melledew, Jenkins, Butler; Sub: Buck, for Rudd, 63 minutes. Scorers: Melledew, Jenkins (2). Attendance: 9,890.

Congratulations to the
'DALE'
and best wishes for the future.

BRADLEYS MUSIC
DRAKE STREET, ROCHDALE
TEL: 44474

We installed the public address system and supplied the organ for the Social Club.

Congratulations!
to the Dale
FROM THE
'Observer'
Your Local Paper for Sports Report and Comment every Wednesday and Saturday

AFTERMATH

However the cheesiest tribute of all, although it probably symbolised the times, came from someone who styled himself the "Bard of Swindon". **Swindon,** for Christ's sake - I think he simply forgot the "AST" after the "B"! Anyway, he penned the following (and the Observer was daft enough to print it) so here goes:

> *My beloved Rochdale,*
> *out of the basement at last.*
> *The 48-year wait is over,*
> *thanks to Melledew's blast.*
> *A toast to the Reverend Gentlemen,*
> *who helped the dream come true.*
> *To goalkeeper Harker,*
> *for letting in so few.*
> *Step forward Jenkins,*
> *well played Leech.*
> *Great defending Ryder,*
> *in a line so tough to breach.*
> *Dashing wing play Whitehead,*
> *prompted well by Parry.*
> *Smith has been a tower of strength,*
> *keeping Spotland hale and hearty.*
> *Ashworth has been another trump,*
> *Butler a continual threat.*
> *Against Southend they were dazzlers all,*
> *destroyers in the fret.*
> *So watch out Fulham and Luton,*
> *now we've hit the top.*
> *We're on our way to the Second,*
> *a year after it's the Kop.*

Presumably on the grounds of taste and public decency laws, there was fortunately no rhyming couplet involving Tony Buck!

ECHOES OF '69

What a season it had been! A post-war club record unbeaten run of fifteen games; Dennis Butler ending the season with sixteen goals, a club record for a winger; only sixteen players used throughout the campaign; and, finally, promotion achieved despite winning only four games away from Spotland. It had been a real roller-coaster of emotions. The pivotal stage for me had been the Christmas period, from the defeat at Swansea to the win at Workington, and centred on three key elements. Firstly, was the impact of Dick Connor's arrival as coach. We didn't think so at the time (his first game was the 3-0 defeat at Swansea) but, thereafter, as he took on more and more responsibility for the fitness and tactics of the team from Len Richley, the results were testimony to his impact. Richley, after all, was more comfortable on the administration side of a football club but the second key element, which Richley himself alluded to after the Southend promotion clincher, was the collective "bollocking" that the team received after the Swansea game. As Richley pointed out it was not because they lost, rather it was the manner of **how** they lost. The third element highlights the impact of one of the unsung heroes of the team, Graham Smith, who was in and out of the side during the first four months of the campaign. In my opinion, it was no mere coincidence that the record-breaking run started at Workington when Smith replaced Radcliffe at right-back, and subsequently kept that position for the rest of the season.

In recognition of his increasing contribution, Dick Connor was promoted to assistant manager on 21st May and, two days later, a Civic Reception was held in honour of the team's achievement at Rochdale Town Hall. Even at this stage there was some dissent in the ranks. The event was personally boycotted by the curmudgeonly Alderman Frank Grant, who believed that spending public money on this kind of recognition of achievement should have been reserved for a team which had actually won a trophy. Later in the month, when the traditional "retained list" of players' registrations was submitted to Football League headquarters, it was revealed that Joe Fletcher, Vince Radcliffe and Matt Tyrie had all been released.

AFTERMATH

At Howarth Cross, the play "Toad of Toad Hall" played to packed audiences and was extremely well received. The author, his voice now having broken completely, was able to lend extra resonance and bass to his solo rendition of the words

"May all his laces tie themselves in knots,
and may his fountain pen make frequent blots!"

as a motley assembly of assorted Stoats, Weasels and Ferrets belted out the toe-tapping ditty **"Down with Toad"**. I am also pleased to report that the Chief Stoat succeeded in keeping his hands off the female members of the cast for the duration of the run, although it was a close thing!

The other highlight of the summer term was the school holiday to France. For my mate John, the first day was not an auspicious one. Getting off the coach at Manchester's Piccadilly Station, from where we would catch the train to London, he managed to crack his duffle bag on the coach steps, thereby shattering his Thermos flask to general merriment as a trail of liquid followed his progress onto the concourse. Things went better for him during the next few hours. After transferring from Euston to Victoria Station, we had a couple of hours to kill so, armed with a London A-Z map, I led a small expedition to Buckingham Palace, despite never having been to London before in my (short) life. Subsequently, we caught the boat train to Folkestone, then ferry to Calais and finally the SNCF train to Paris. Safely arrived at our hotel, we were allowed to go out and do our own thing and find something to eat for a couple of hours. John, Barry Lord and I found ourselves sat outside a nice bistro, on some leafy boulevard, where we ordered bottles of Coke and chicken and chips (or poulet et frites if you prefer). The meal was very nice and, as we headed back to our hotel, we thought that was the last of it. Well, for Barry and me, it was. Unfortunately, John's literally came back to haunt him during the night, although, looking on the bright side, he did succeed in finding a use for the bidet. Sadly, it was beyond my linguistic skills at the time to explain to the receptionist, next morning, that the bidet was terminally blocked and would need plunging!

These disasters apart, we enjoyed a cracking good holiday. After a couple of days sightseeing all over Paris, and practising our schoolboy French, none too convincingly, we undertook the long train journey to Biarritz in the extreme South-West of France. One of our party, Eddy Kleijdis, somehow persuaded a refreshment vendor to sell him a cheap bottle of champagne. This had the effect of making him very lively for the first hour of the journey but he slept right through the other six. Maybe these were the correct tactics in those pre-Gameboy and Walkman days. Frankly, the attraction of knock-out whist and "Fizz-Buzz" starts to pale after the first couple of hours. After the first day, when disappointingly it rained, the sun "cracked the flags" for the next six days, during which we spent most of our time on the beach and in the sea. Everybody got sunburnt after the first day and all you could hear from our hotel rooms were screams of agony as we applied Ambre Solaire after-sun to each other's backs. We tried to be adventurous with the food, but we were confounded by the hotel serving us soup each day before our evening meal; a kind of minestrone, if I'm not mistaken. Nothing wrong with that, I hear you say. Well no. Except that it was the **same** soup each night, augmented by a few of the previous day's leftovers. As the week wore on, we started to recognise the shapes of certain floating pieces that we had first seen a couple of days previously! Lovely! We made up for this, however, by the constant supply of syrupy doughnuts available from the beachside café, where we would adjourn for games of table football and marvel at how French kids were so much better at "whiffle" than "us Brits". The Headmaster, Jack Kershaw, had brought his family on the holiday and I earned his displeasure one day on the beach by swearing at his son who, a

AFTERMATH

couple of years younger than us, had been annoying all and sundry by kicking sand over people whilst they were sunbathing. "Jack the Whack" didn't actually hear me saying *"bugger off you annoying little git"*, but he went straight to tell his dad. What a grass! Mr. Kershaw told me that I had "used inappropriate language which might have damaged the reputation of the school" - I just wish I could have introduced him at that very minute to Terry Melling! Incidentally, the rat of a son was called Andrew - you might know him as the TV presenter and former Radio One DJ, Andy Kershaw. I much preferred his sister, and fellow Radio One presenter, Liz, whose Form Prefect I would become in my last year at Greenhill, some years later.

When we got back to sunny (?) Rochdale, I was amazed at how interested people were to hear about my trip to France. I realised that I was the first person from my immediate family to visit a foreign country (if you don't include Wales, Scotland or even the Isle of Man!) but friends and neighbours were equally curious. Today we take foreign travel totally for granted and it is really weird to look back only (!) thirty-three years and see the fundamental shift in our expectation levels.

However, now that we were back, our thoughts could turn to the challenge ahead of Third Division football. Exciting times were around the corner for the Dale; we would humble a full-strength Everton side (who would go on to win the championship that year) 4-3 in a pre-season friendly; after eight (yes 8!) successive wins we would briefly top the Division in November, before injuries ravaged the small squad over the second half of the season; and, looking still further forward, would be the epic FA Cup "giant-killing" of First Division Coventry City.

All of these hugely enjoyable experiences were still some way off in the future (along with Boddington's Bitter, Chester's Mild and a more intimate knowledge of the female form and psyche!) but season 1968-69 and the associated memories will

ECHOES OF '69

live with me forever. If you've enjoyed sharing these memories with me, then I'm genuinely pleased because I've certainly enjoyed dredging them up! Have I reached any conclusions from this exercise in introspection? Yes! My Dad was right all along - I was, and remain, a daft pillock!

CHEERS!!!

APPENDIX 1

"Where are they now?"

You will recognise, my boy, the first sign of old age; it is when you go out in the streets of London and realise for the first time how young the policemen look.
Seymour Hicks (1871-1948)

So what became of the heroes of yesteryear in the decades following the momentous season 1968-69?

CHRIS HARKER

Chris stayed with the club for just one more season but again played in all 46 league games (as he had in 68/9) to earn the highly unusual accolade of being an ever-present throughout his period at the club, recording a total of 92 league appearances. He left with manager Len Richley to join Darlington as their trainer, before joining Stockport County as player-coach. After drifting out of football, he proceeded to spend 25 years working as a fitter/joiner for Magnet in his roots in Darlington and is now employed as caretaker of the Hummersknot Comprehensive School.

GRAHAM SMITH

Graham would eventually go on to become Rochdale's record-holder for League appearances, notching up 317 (including one as a substitute), scoring just two goals, before he was released at the end of the disastrous 1973-4 season. He was awarded a joint testimonial along with fellow stalwarts Dennis Butler and Reg Jenkins and then joined Stockport County, where he stayed for a further five years. He held the position of player-coach at non-leaguers Buxton and Thackley, and subsequently has concentrated on running the family plumbing business TA Smith and Sons in

ECHOES OF '69

Pudsey, Yorkshire (with occasional scouting activities for Southampton).

DEREK RYDER

Derek would leave the Dale at the end of the '71/72 season to join Southport after amassing a total of 168 league appearances and also scoring just two goals. He left the game to work as a sales representative for Scottish & Newcastle Breweries, and subsequently Tetley's, before settling as a self-employed gardener in his native Leeds. Soccer, beer and gardening - sounds like a recipe for an enjoyable life to me!

VINNY LEECH

Vinny's career would be brought to a premature end following a serious knee injury and he left Rochdale after the 1970/1 season, briefly playing non-league football for Fleetwood before finally hanging up his boots. He totalled 60 League appearances for the Dale, scoring just once. After running a series of guest houses on the Fylde coast in conjunction with his good lady wife, Vinny now assists in the management of his wife's hair-dressing salon in Poulton-le-Fylde and plays lots of golf at the Knott End club.

COLIN PARRY

Colin was another long-serving player who eventually left the club at the end of season '71/2 (joining then non-league Macclesfield Town) after playing in 156 League games during which he too scored just a single goal. He has subsequently spent the best part of thirty years as a miller at Nelstrop's Flour Mill in his home-town Stockport (and, allegedly, has a profound distaste for talking to adolescent boys on the upper deck of Rochdale buses!).

JOE ASHWORTH

Joe clocked up 133 League appearances for Rochdale, scoring a relatively-prolific (for a Dale defender of that time!) three goals

ECHOES OF '69

before his career was wrecked by a severe Achilles tendon injury. He entered the Prison Service, working in Hull, Strangeways and Newhall, before crippling arthritis forced his retirement in 1997 and he subsequently underwent hip replacement surgery. Sadly, "Big Joe" passed away in the summer of 2002.

NORMAN WHITEHEAD

Norman would leave Rochdale in March 1972 in a £10,000 move to Rotherham United (which also saw Lee Brogden travelling in the opposite direction). His eventual tally for the Dale was 156 League games during which he found the net on eleven occasions. He went on to play for Chester, Grimsby Town, Bangor City and Rhyl before returning to his native Merseyside where he worked on the Mersey Ferry Service. He is now a maintenance operative in a Wallasey nursing home.

BILLY RUDD

"Little Billy" was transferred to Bury for £5,000 in June 1970 (in the days when Bury actually had £5,000!) having played in 108 League games and scored eight goals. He linked up again with Bob Stokoe in 1978 as Blackpool's reserve team coach before setting up his own decorating business in Bury. He has also done some part-time scouting for Aston Villa.

TONY BUCK

The Dale's record signing at the time at £5,000, Tony would make 85 League appearances scoring 29 goals in the process. He never seemed to fully recover from a broken leg (sustained in a collision with the sinisterly-named Reading goalkeeper, Steve Death) and, after playing for Northampton and Bradford City, would eventually be forced out of the game by a serious knee injury. He now lives in Northampton and has worked for a number of years as a service controller for Axus.

ECHOES OF '69

REG JENKINS

"Big Reg", as he will always be affectionately known by the public of Rochdale, remains the club's record goalscorer with 119 goals in 305 League games. He returned to his native south-west in 1973 to join Falmouth Town and then served Millbrook as player and manager for over twenty years. Before retiring in 1990, Reg worked as a shipwright in Plymouth docks.

DENNIS BUTLER

Dennis was forced out of the game through injury in May 1973 after completing 156 League games for Rochdale during which he netted 36 times. Coaching roles subsequently took him to Bury, Port Vale and Swindon Town before he returned to the town to run Bamford Post Office. He still lives close to Spotland, now working for Rochdale Council in the Education department.

STEVIE MELLEDEW

Stevie, the most famous person ever to work for Whipp & Bourne and the discovery of Dale doyen Tom Nichol, was sold to champions Everton shortly after promotion for a then record outgoing Rochdale fee of £15,000. He subsequently joined Aldershot, Bury and Crewe Alexandra before rejoining the Dale in 1976, completing 174 League games in total during which he notched 35 goals. After managing a variety of non-league clubs, he is now Assistant Chief Youth Development Scout for Reading F.C.

VINCE RADCLIFFE

Vince scored once for Rochdale in his 26 League appearances before joining Kings Lynn in 1969. He subsequently emigrated to Australia and played for a number of clubs there, eventually coaching the Sorrento team. He now lives in Daniella, where he works as a Sales Manager in the confectionery industry.

ECHOES OF '69

JOE FLETCHER

Joe scored 21 goals in 57 League appearances for the Dale before joining Grimsby Town in July 1969. After spells with Barrow, Chorley and Wigan Athletic, he also emigrated to Australia and spent three years with Hakoah. Returning to England, he served with Mossley, Macclesfield and New Mills. He still lives in Manchester where he runs his own company, Eurofans and Accessories.

MATT TYRIE

Matt was released in the summer of 1969 without ever playing a League game for the team. After playing for a variety of junior Scottish clubs, he took up refereeing. Now living in Carluke, he has worked for the Prudential since 1979.

HUGHEN RILEY

Local lad, and self-proclaimed celebrity, Hughie scored twelve goals in his 93 League appearances for Rochdale and was another of Tom Nichol's boys. After joining Crewe in December 1971, he went on to play for Bury, Bournemouth, Dorchester and Weymouth. He has since been the licensee of various public houses "down south" and currently runs the Hen & Chicken Inn at Froyle near Alton in Hampshire.

BOB STOKOE

Bob left Rochdale to join Carlisle United in October 1968 before managing Blackpool and, most famously, Sunderland when they beat the all-conquering Leeds United side 1-0 to win the FA Cup in 1973. Amongst a variety of other clubs, he briefly returned to manage the Dale again during 1979-80. Now retired, he lives in his native North-East.

ECHOES OF '69

LEN RICHLEY

Len resigned in February 1970 and subsequently managed Darlington. He then became Newcastle United's Chief Scout and remained in his native North-East until his untimely death in October 1980.

DICK CONNOR

Dick took over from Len Richley and led the Dale to their highest post-war League position. He too went on to manage Darlington before returning to Rochdale in a coaching capacity. Now retired, he lives in Hebburn in the North-East.

Sadly, I have to confess that I haven't a f***ing clue what happened to that **** Terry Melling!!! If any of the readers happen to be in contact with him, please pass on my best regards!

APPENDIX 2

The Statistics

"He uses statistics as a drunken man uses lampposts - for support rather than for illumination"
Andrew Lang (1844-1912)

FOOTBALL LEAGUE DIVISION 4
1968-69 Final Table

	P	HOME W	D	L	F	A	AWAY W	D	L	F	A	Pts
Doncaster Rovers	46	13	8	2	42	18	8	9	6	23	22	59
Halifax Town	46	15	5	3	36	18	5	12	6	17	19	57
ROCHDALE	**46**	**14**	**7**	**2**	**47**	**11**	**4**	**13**	**6**	**21**	**24**	**56**
Bradford City	46	11	10	2	36	18	7	10	6	29	28	56
Darlington	46	11	6	6	40	26	6	12	5	22	19	52
Colchester United	46	12	8	3	31	17	8	4	11	26	36	52
Southend United	46	15	3	5	51	21	4	10	9	27	40	51
Lincoln City	46	13	6	4	38	19	4	11	8	16	33	51
Wrexham	46	13	7	3	41	22	5	7	11	20	30	50
Swansea Town	46	11	8	4	35	20	8	3	12	23	34	49
Brentford	46	12	7	4	40	24	6	5	12	24	41	48
Workington	46	8	11	4	24	17	7	6	10	16	26	47
Port Vale	46	12	8	3	33	15	4	6	13	13	31	46
Chester	46	12	4	7	43	24	4	9	10	33	42	45
Aldershot	46	13	3	7	42	23	6	4	13	24	43	45
Scunthorpe United	46	10	5	8	28	22	8	3	12	33	38	44
Exeter City	46	11	8	4	45	24	5	3	15	21	41	43
Peterborough United	46	8	9	6	32	23	5	7	11	28	34	42
Notts County	46	10	8	5	33	22	2	10	11	15	35	42
Chesterfield	46	7	7	9	24	22	6	8	9	19	28	41
York City	46	12	8	3	36	25	2	3	18	17	50	39
Newport County	46	9	9	5	31	26	2	5	16	18	48	36
Grimsby Town	46	5	7	11	25	31	4	8	11	22	38	33
Bradford Park Avenue	46	5	8	10	19	34	0	2	21	13	72	20

ECHOES OF '69

APPEARANCES IN SEASON 1968/69

(Substitute appearances in parentheses)
LEAGUE

Player	APPS	GOALS
ASHWORTH	39	1
BUCK	15(2)	8
BUTLER	44(2)	16
FLETCHER	8(2)	2
HARKER	46	0
JENKINS	28(5)	13
LEECH	44	0
MELLEDEW	25(4)	12
MELLING	20	8
PARRY	45	0
RADCLIFFE	26	1
RILEY	1	0
RUDD	46	4
RYDER	46	0
SMITH	31(1)	1
WHITEHEAD	41(1)	2

COMPARATIVE ATTENDANCE RECORDS

SEASON	TOTAL SPECTATORS	AVERAGE PER GAME	GROSS RECEIPTS
49/50	200,295	9,104	£14,981
64/65	112,633	4,691	£14,532
65/66	84,798	3,140	£13,154
66/67	60,761	2,430	£10,171
67/68	62,348	2,398	£11,000
68/69	134,477	5,172	£26,000

68/69
Average League Gate 5,420 (previous season 2,364)
Total Home League 124,681 (previous season 54,392)
Highest - 13,266 v Halifax (previous season 4,413 v Bradford City)